Information Architecture

The Design and Integration of
Information Spaces

Second Edition

Synthesis Lectures on Information Concepts, Retrieval, and Services

Editor

Gary Marchionini, *University of North Carolina, Chapel Hill*

Synthesis Lectures on Information Concepts, Retrieval, and Services publishes short books on topics pertaining to information science and applications of technology to information discovery, production, distribution, and management. Potential topics include: data models, indexing theory and algorithms, classification, information architecture, information economics, privacy and identity, scholarly communication, bibliometrics and webometrics, personal information management, human information behavior, digital libraries, archives and preservation, cultural informatics, information retrieval evaluation, data fusion, relevance feedback, recommendation systems, question answering, natural language processing for retrieval, text summarization, multimedia retrieval, multilingual retrieval, and exploratory search.

Information Architecture

The Design and Integration of

Information Spaces

Second Edition

Wei Ding
Consumer Financial Protection Bureau (CFPB)
Xia Lin
Drexel University
Michael Zarro
Project Management Institute

SYNTHESIS LECTURES ON INFORMATION CONCEPTS, RETRIEVAL, AND SERVICES #56

ABSTRACT

Information Architecture is about organizing and simplifying information, designing and integrating information spaces/systems, and creating ways for people to find and interact with information content. Its goal is to help people understand and manage information and make the right decisions accordingly. This updated and revised edition of the book looks at integrated information spaces in the web context and beyond, with a focus on putting theories and principles into practice.

In the ever-changing social, organizational, and technological contexts, information architects not only design individual information spaces (e.g., websites, software applications, and mobile devices), but also tackle strategic aggregation and integration of multiple information spaces across websites, channels, modalities, and platforms. Not only do they create predetermined navigation pathways, but they also provide tools and rules for people to organize information on their own and get connected with others.

Information architects work with multi-disciplinary teams to determine the user experience strategy based on user needs and business goals, and make sure the strategy gets carried out by following the user-centered design (UCD) process via close collaboration with others. Drawing on the authors' extensive experience as HCI researchers, User Experience Design practitioners, and Information Architecture instructors, this book provides a balanced view of the IA discipline by applying theories, design principles, and guidelines to IA and UX practices. It also covers advanced topics such as iterative design, UX decision support, and global and mobile IA considerations. Major revisions include moving away from a web-centric view toward multi-channel, multi-device experiences. Concepts such as responsive design, emerging design principles, and user-centered methods such as Agile, Lean UX, and Design Thinking are discussed and related to IA processes and practices.

KEYWORDS

information architecture, user experience design, content management, user-centered design methodology, interaction design, usability, global IA, mobile IA, navigation design, design for persuasion and engagement, search interface design, enterprise IA

Contents

Preface

The term Information Architecture (IA) was coined by a brick-and-mortar architect, Richard Wurman, in the early 1970s as a profession of "gathering, organizing, and presenting information." The World Wide Web accelerated the information explosion and created the real need for the profession to help more people find and manage useful information online. However, the debate on Little IA vs. Big IA never seems to have settled. Some people argue the information architects (aka little IAs) are only associated with taxonomy, metadata, thesaurus, and other "information findability" related tasks. Meanwhile, others believe that IAs (aka big IAs) are responsible for synthesizing all data and information from the business and users, and crafting user experience vision and design solutions. This book holds the "Big IA" view and sees "Little IAs" being one of the IA specialties.

The authors believe that the continuous evolution of the information spaces supported by the web and cloud technologies makes it possible to deliver more sophisticated interactions and user activities; the level of depth and breadth of the corresponding information architecture work has increased accordingly. At the same time, it brings the convergence of multiple disciplines as User Experience (UX) Design, including usability/human factors, interaction design, graphical design, information architecture, and many more.

This convergence calls for a higher level of seamless collaboration among all the disciplines, but it does not eliminate the need for dedicated IA work. Instead, information architecture work spreads from traditional web design to digital devices, apps, medical devices, automobiles, and many other places. Information architects are part of the TEAM determining the user experience strategy based on user needs and business goals, and make sure the strategy gets carried out via the collaboration of multiple disciplines by following the user-centered design (UCD) process.

Drawing on the authors' extensive experience as User Experience Design practitioners, HCI researchers, and information architecture instructors, this book outlines a balanced view of the IA discipline by connecting a practitioner's real-world experience and IA/UX practices to human information behavioral theories, design principles, and guidelines. In addition to demonstrating the conventional IA deliverables, techniques, and tools, this book emphasizes that information architecture is about the design and integration of information spaces (both digital and physical) that are bigger than and beyond the web.

USES OF THE BOOK

This book is a result of our teaching of a graduate-level course on information architecture at Drexel University for a number of years. The content has been constantly updated to incorporate the latest developments in the field. In this revised edition, we follow the trend in IA, centering less on web-specific design details and more on design patterns, themes, and building for an information-centric future. Three chapters of this revision are completely new (Chapter 2, 8, and 9) and every other chapter has been significantly revised. Eight years between the two editions (2009–2017) is considered a long time in the short history of IA. This new edition will help document the changes and bring the reader to the new developments and new ways of thinking as IA evolves. The objective of the course is to introduce fundamental IA concepts, theories, processes and techniques, in the context of user-centered design, to graduate students majoring in Library and Information Science as well as in Information Systems. We cannot stress more that the essential point of learning for this course is to "learn by doing." This text is intended to encourage those learning activities. As the book was originally written as lecture notes, we believe it is most suitable to be used as textbook for similar courses in other schools. The key features of the book include concise discussions structured around each topic and the balanced coverage of theoretical and practical issues. Drexel's courses are quarter courses that typically include 10 lecture weeks. We have conveniently structured the book in 10 chapters, one for each week. The content for each week can be easily expanded when used for a semester course.

User experience practitioners should also find this book useful and inspiring. We hope this book can help bridge the gap between the community of practice and academia.

STRUCTURE OF THE BOOK

The book covers the following topics.

- Information Architecture: Definition and Evolution

  Chapter 1 discusses the definition of information architecture in the context of integrated information spaces, its impact on the way people interact with information, and IA's relation to other UX disciplines. Chapter 2 takes a historical perspective to examine the evolution of the web and identifies new challenges and opportunities for the IA discipline in the context of an era of highly integrated information spaces.

- IA Processes and Methodology

  Chapter 3 introduces IA steps and workflows in the context of the User-Centered Design methodology, which is the prerequisite for conducting any information architecture practices.

- IA Foundations and Design Principles

  As the core of the book, Chapters 4, 5, 6, 7, and 8 are dedicated to the IA key concepts and foundations, including information organization and navigation; human information behavior and the corresponding design implications; as well as interaction design patterns, principles, and best practices. These chapters incorporate the latest developments in the field, like responsive design and mobile, and reflect the current state of knowledge for usability researchers and user experience design professionals.

- IA in Practice

  In Chapter 9, the design and development team is discussed. Frameworks like Agile development and Lean UX are related to the ideas presented in previous chapters. We present a UX decision support framework that can be used to make IA decisions, reduce uncertainty, and provide support for team discussions about IA research and design.

- The Future of Information Architecture

  Chapter 10 identifies IA trends and future directions, including growing global considerations, and urges IA researchers and practitioners to work together to continue to promote and grow the discipline. The chapter ends with a revisit of the IA definition used throughout the book.

CHAPTER 1

Information Architecture: Definitions and Scopes

Information architecture is an exciting area of study that is growing in importance in academics, industry, as well as everyday life. As we all interact with technology everyday—websites, search engines, mobile apps, smart car apps, or smart home devices, why do we have a good experience with some of them but not others? Who creates and designs these things that make our life pleasant (or miserable)? How can we structure information in a usable way so that we can all find it when we need it? Clearly, it is valuable to study the "space" between technologies, human cognitive abilities, information content, and the context of use. Enter Information Architecture (IA), which now is becoming an emerging interdisciplinary field that is rooted in website design, information design, user experience design, information organization, information access, and information use.

1.1 DEFINITIONS OF INFORMATION ARCHITECTURE

Like many other emerging disciplines, there exist many definitions of information architecture. Let's start with a look at a few examples of the definitions first.

1.1.1 WURMAN'S DEFINITION OF INFORMATION ARCHITECT

One cannot talk about information architecture without mentioning Richard Saul Wurman, who coined the term "Information Architecture" or, at least, brought it to wide attention in the 1970s. Wurman was trained as an architect and skilled at graphical design, but "making information understandable" has been "the singular passion of his life." He sees the problems of gathering, organizing, and presenting information as closely analogous to the problems an architect faces in designing a building that will serve the needs of its occupants. His definition of information architects emphasizes the *organization* and *presentation* of information (Wurman, 1996).

> "(1) The individual who organizes the patterns inherent in data, making the complex clear. (2) A person who creates the structure or map of information which allows others to find their personal paths to knowledge. (3) The emerging 21st century professional occupation addressing the needs of the age focused upon clarity, human understanding, and the science of the organization of information."

Wurman explains, "I mean architect as used in the words architect of foreign policy. I mean architect as in the creating of systemic, structural, and orderly principles to make something work." The job of information architects is more focused on "making the complex clear" through better organization and presentation of information.

1.1.2   ROSENFIELD AND MORVILLE'S DEFINITION

While Wurman insightfully bridged *information* with *architecture*, it is Louis Rosenfield and Peter Morville who brought information architecture to the mainstream with their popular "polar bear" book on information architecture (2015). Now in the fourth edition (with Jorge Arango as an additional author), the authors took a multi-perspective approach to define information architecture.

- The structural design of shared information environments.

- The synthesis of organization, labeling, search, and navigation systems within digital, physical, and cross-channel ecosystems.

- The art and science of shaping information products and experience to support usability and findability, and understanding.

- An emerging discipline and community of practice focused on bringing principles of design and architecture to the digital landscape.

The first bullet is a very broad perspective on information environments with an emphasis on "structural design." The second bullet specifies the scope of information architecture in the digital and physical information space as well as the cross-channels. The third highlights the relationship between information architecture, usability, findability, and understanding of information. The spirit of IA as a discipline is well represented in the fourth bullet—bringing principles of *design* and *architecture* to the *digital landscape*. It also explains why information architecture became a discipline in the web environment, although the IA related work existed long before the World Wide Web era. And it continues to evolve.

1.1.3   PERVASIVE INFORMATION ARCHITECTURE

We live in a world of complex information environments. Besides websites, more information devices such as televisions, car dashboards, and mobile apps become more interactive and linked to each other, and social media becomes more prevalent—people are using, creating, and sharing more and more information in multiple channels or cross-channels. In their book, *Pervasive Information Architecture*, Resmini and Rosati (2011) emphasize that, as the information environment evolves, "information architecture was moving into uncharted territories, becoming a boundary practice whose contributions were crucial where complexity, unfamiliarity, and information overload stood in the way of the user, regardless of the very nature of the environment being designed. Information architecture was moving beyond the confines of the web." Thus, their definition of information architecture underscores information architecture as a process and service design, involving designing multi-channel and cross-channel user experience.

1.1.4   ENTERPRISE INFORMATION ARCHITECTURE

Information architecture has a special meaning to organizations and institutions. In addition to organizing and using information, IA in organizations involves architecture and implementation and management of key information assets, thus a special term, Enterprise Information Architecture. Newman et al. (2008) define *Enterprise Information Architecture* as "part of the enterprise architecture process that describes—through a set of requirements, principles and models—the current state, future state, and guidance necessary to flexibly share and exchange information assets to achieve effective enterprise change." In their article, they further explain each component of this definition and outline challenges of information architecture in the enterprise environment. Essentially, the roles of information architects in enterprise include designing, integrating, and aggregating information spaces/systems and facilitating information sharing and collaboration in order to foster enterprise culture, improve productivity, ensure quality of custom service and competitive advantage, and support business profitable growth and innovation. Enterprise information architecture itself has become an important domain of study in the business world.

1.1.5   THE DEFINITION USED IN THIS BOOK

In the above, we provide snapshots of different definitions of information architecture, from pre-web, web-centric, to the post-web era, and to the enterprise environment. A common theme of the evolution is from information-centric to user-centric, thus the definition we use in this book:

> Information architecture is about organizing and simplifying information for its intended users; designing, integrating, and aggregating information spaces to create usable systems or interfaces; creating ways for people to find, understand, exchange and manage information; and, therefore, stay on top of information and make the right decisions.

Information architects not only design individual information spaces (e.g., websites, software, applications, intranets) but also tackle strategic aggregation and integration of multiple information spaces, including all channels, modalities, and platforms. They not only organize information but also simplify information for better understanding. Finally, the goal of IA design is not only to support people to find information but to manage and use information.

This definition serves as the common theme for all the chapters/topics in this book. At the end of the book, we will revisit this definition again.

1.2   FROM WEB DESIGN TO INFORMATION ARCHITECTURE

The rise and rapid evolution of the web has brought many opportunities and challenges for users and designers. The user population has grown exponentially from originally academic users to virtually everybody, from young children to elderly people. User needs have expanded from viewing information only to taking actions and contributing to the site's information content and architecture. At the same time, user expectations of the web, websites, and search engines have risen accordingly. For example, more people expect search engines to be answer engines—giving the answer right away instead of just showing pages that have the potential to provide answers; people assume that any answer should be available on the web. The web is no longer just made up of hyperlinks for people to browse; it is the place for people to hop on as a routine, conduct daily activities, connect with others, and experience and influence the world.

As the breadth and depth of people's interaction with the web evolves, the boundaries between the physical world and cyber space are blurring. The needed information architecture work organizing information—connecting information objects and intended users, identifying pathways for people to navigate, creating tools and rules for people to organize information on their own and collaborate with their others, and integrating and aggregating various information spaces, applications, platforms, and channels—becomes so critical and ubiquitous. At the same time, because cyber space is so intertwined with every aspect of people's lives, information architecture alone can no longer fulfill all the sophisticated user needs—the information needs to be relevant and understandable; the space needs to be organized and explorable; the interaction needs to be efficient and engaging; the overall experience needs to be pleasant, effective, engaging, and trustworthy.

To accomplish these goals, information architects work closely with many other disciplines to ensure all the issues are taken care of and all challenges are met. Only when all the related disciplines fully leverage their expertise and skillsets, can the overall user experience be made possible. This brings the convergence of multiple disciplines as User Experience (UX) Design (Garrett, 2002), including usability/human factors engineering, interaction design, graphical design, information architecture, and many more.

1.3   INFORMATION ARCHITECTURE AND RELATED DISCIPLINES

Although many of the above-mentioned disciplines originated in different contexts aiming to solve different problems, the evolvement and expansion of the web brings them together. *Usability engineering* is primarily concerned with human computer interaction, and its goal is to make sure the user interface allows the user to accomplish their tasks effectively, efficiently, and satisfactorily. Usability engineering started before the web era by focusing on the usability of software user interfaces. The web explosion made it applicable to all web applications and websites.

Information science is a very broad interdisciplinary field concerning theories, applications, and technologies related to creation, organization, retrieval, and use of information. It is also the field where Rosenfeld and Morville started developing information architecture methodologies for creating content organization, navigation, and labeling systems. Subdomains of information science that are most relevant to information architecture include users' information needs and information-seeking behaviors, information organization and retrieval, and understanding the content and context of information.

Human factors engineering is the discipline of applying what is known about human capabilities and limitations to the design of products, processes, systems, and work environments. Originating from designs of airplane pilot's dashboards and hardware or physical products, human factors professionals obviously now apply their expertise to digital platforms.

Interaction design is a broad concept that goes beyond computer interface design. Any design that involves people's input and the product's response can be categorized as interaction design, including home appliances, electronics, and even electronic car dashboards. However, the interactivity between the user and the system in software user interface and web applications is so rich and omnipresent that we cannot talk about web design and user experience without mentioning interaction design. In cyber space, it is getting very hard to separate *information architecture* from *interaction design* because they are both concerned with defining the system and user behavior, giving users controls to make sense of things, take actions, and to accomplish certain things. Some people try to differentiate the two by emphasizing that interaction designers can show the dynamic interactions between the user and the system. Information architects can do the same thing if needed. It all depends what can best demonstrate the user experience concepts. People in different organizations may get different titles, but the truth of the matter is certain people on the project teams need to worry about the functional behavior of the system and of the user. These people are doing information architecture and interaction design type of work.

Recently there is a school of thought that argues that IA is not a profession. "There are no information architects, and there are no interaction designers. There are only user experience designers" (Morville et al., 2015). In our perspective, this is not to deny the existence of the information architecture discipline but a desire to strengthen it. The important message in this statement is, though, to call for synergy augmentation between two sub-communities that really belong to the same big community. In practice, the terms "user experience architects" and "information architects" are sometimes used interchangeably. Rima Reda, an "experience architect" (2014). described the connections between experience and architecture, pointing out the many common grounds, including "visual problem solving," which spans several disciplines no matter the label.

Although interaction design and information architecture came from different contexts and backgrounds, they are both landing on the same web wonderland and beyond. They both have been transformed because of today's technological and social contexts where neither group had previous experience.

Visual design does not only concern itself with the aesthetical aspect of the information space and the user interface. Good visual design clarifies communication and makes the information and interaction easier to understand. Visual designers make the best use of the visual language, such as colors, shapes, layouts, spacing, alignments, and styles, to help reinforce the communication between the system and the user, express emotions, trust, and personalities of the site or application and engage the user in a positive way. Visual designers bring great principles, theories, and best practices accumulated in the print world. By closely working with other disciplines, they help transform design concepts to pixel perfect screens.

Finally, *information design* is another area (Jacobson, 2000) that overlaps with information architecture. While it may not be an established field of study, information design has been used interchangeably with *visual design* or *graphical design* with an emphasis on designing displays for the content or structures of information, thus more closely related to the field of *information visualization*.

In this book, we argue that information architecture is one of the most important elements in user experience design, and information architecture work serves as the glue to stick all the related puzzle pieces together. From a user-centered design process perspective, information architects get involved in the process from the beginning to the end.

- They work with the business to help establish business vision and strategy about the website, the intranet, or the digital workspace.

- They work with user researchers/usability engineers to identify the right research methods and determine the research goals and objectives. Also, they digest research findings and transform them into specific design concepts.

- They work hand in hand with interaction designers to define the interaction model and system behavior. They determine the system functionality and connections between information objects and workflows.

- They work with visual designers to create user experience visioning screens upfront and later convert design concepts into final designs with all visual details in place.

- They also work with development and testing teams to make sure the design gets implemented and functions as intended.

That being said, we think information architecture has had and will continue to have a great role to play in user experience design practices. As information access, sharing, creation, organization, management, and consumption become ubiquitous, the collaboration among all disciplines will become even more critical and necessary.

1.4   SUMMARY

Information architecture is a field with growing importance across all walks of life, as boundaries between the physical world and information spaces blur. IA can be defined several ways, we define it for this book in terms of designing, organizing, and integrating information spaces so that people experience positive outcomes—being informed and making good decisions. Information architects work closely with other professionals, bringing together the pieces of the puzzle needed to create meaningful, functional, and beautiful information spaces.

CHAPTER 2

Information Architecture and Evolving Information Spaces

Online and other digital information spaces are increasingly integrated into everyday life. Today, over three billion people around the globe are connected to the internet, including a large majority in developed countries and an increasing number in developing countries (ICT Data and Statistics Division, 2015). It seems that more and more time is spent "online" as formerly offline activities (like depositing a check or hailing a cab) move to websites and mobile apps. Cellular networks, WiFi, and mobile devices keep connections alive 24 hours a day; while broadband connectivity lets the 1's and 0's that carry information fly around the globe at the speed of light. Mobile, wearables, sensors, artificial intelligence, and "the internet of things" are quickly becoming a bigger part of our lives.

Although it only has a short history, the content and look of the World Wide Web (the web, WWW) and internet, as well as information space design and digital technologies in general, have all gone through several generations of changes. In this chapter we will highlight major changes in this evolution—from a domain of the select few to the connected world many of us live in today, with ubiquitous connectivity and where freedom of internet access is considered a basic human right and a "driving force" in development (United Nations General Assembly, 2012).

Activities in information spaces today can be distributed across time and space, where previously they were bound to a time and location; "formerly clear lines are fading away—between online and offline, internal and external, owned and shared, customer and user, social and business" (Guenther, 2013, p. 10). Examples of this include the following:

- Patrons previously went to the library and retrieved physical books for a short borrowing period. Now, patrons can borrow eBooks online.

- Shoppers browsed the displays at a department store, what was called "window shopping." Now, shoppers can order almost anything online.

- Children used a modem to connect over the family telephone line and signed off so their parents could make a phone call. Now, many homes have dedicated broadband internet access.

In the previous edition of this book, we anticipated the "always on" world that includes the web, mobile apps, social media, medical sensors, home automation devices, and more. Today, integrated information spaces highlight the need for information architects (IAs) to take into account multi-channel use (e.g. mobile apps and desktop), designing for the benefits and limitations each provides. For example, mobile phones include GPS location services that can enhance the usefulness of an app, "show me restaurants nearby," but are limited by the screen size. Desktop computers, on the other hand, have large screens that support word processing and graphic design, but are unlikely used by a hungry person while they are walking through a city.

Information spaces are pervasive and inter-connected (Resmini and Rosati, 2011), accessible anytime and anywhere. Therefore, IAs should work to maximize the benefits, while minimizing limitations, inherent in each channel or device—a task that can sometimes entail what seems like multiple IA for one project. Ideas like responsive design (Marcotte, 2011) help maintain a cohesive experience while maintaining learnability and findability across devices and channels. Although this chapter looks back at past developments, we also see new areas like voice and automated assistants becoming a part of IA in the future.

2.1   FROM THE WEB TO INTEGRATED INFORMATION SPACES

According to W3C World Wide Web Consortium, the first general release of WWW happened on May 17, 1991 (2000). Since then, the web has grown exponentially, with people and devices connecting to each other at an increasing rate while creating, sharing, and consuming information. The web experience was once mostly static content delivered to a user at a computer workstation. Now, interactive content delivered to the user on the device of their choosing is often the norm.

2.1.1   FROM FOUNDATION TO INTEGRATION

Early in its history the web was primarily meant for read-only access, where the majority of users consumed information created by relatively few. The overall arc has moved toward more interaction and creation, demonstrated by social media, blogs/wikis, online office applications, and more. These capabilities increased the utility of web-based technologies, and helped create our "information society" with a "profound impression on the way the world functions" (Executive Secretariat of the World Summit on the Information Society, 2005).

An information society is one where functions of business, education, healthcare, government, and other critical areas exist largely in information spaces. We feel this is a fair description of the state of affairs in many parts of the world. The information society developed over the years through many generations of the web, starting with the technological foundation and resulting in today's integrated era.

Generations

The web has undergone several transitions since its release: from a foundational era where many of the "core" internet technologies were invented and available to those in the know, to the more static but publicly available web1.0, the more dynamic web2.0, and highly interactive "integrated" eras. Below we provide a generalized timeline with selected technology examples that highlight each timeframe.

Table 2.1: Technology development highlights marking eras of internet/web, and related technologies	
Internet- and Web-related Technologies	**Generation**
Modems, packet switching, wide area network, ARPAnet (precursor to the internet), data packets sent between computers, email, handheld mobile (cellular) phones, ethernet, TCP/IP specifications released, the term "Internet" coined, world wide web (WWW, the web) created at CERN	Foundation The domain of scientists and researchers 1958–1990
High Performance Computing and Communication Act of 1991 (origins of the joke that Al Gore invents the internet), WWW opens to public, America Online (AOL), MOSAIC web browser, Netscape web browser, Yahoo!, Amazon.com, MP3s, Internet Explorer web browser, Macromedia/Adobe Flash, Opera web browser, Apache open source web server, Javascript/CSS, Craigslist, GPS made available for civilian uses, WiFi, Netflix, Google, Paypal, Bluetooth	Web1.0 The web opens to the public 1990–1998
Blogs, Blackberry mobile device, RSS, Pandora music streaming, Wikipedia, Napster, Xbox and Playstation online gaming, Firefox web browser, MySpace, Wordpress blogging platform, Delicious social tagging, Skype, Yelp, Second Life, Flickr, Facebook, Youtube, Google Docs, Twitter	Web2.0 The social web, and mobile beginnings 1998–2006
Amazon Web Services (Cloud Computing), SaaS, iPhone released, Chrome web browser, Android mobile OS, Apple App Store, Android market, Roku streaming device, Instagram, iPad, Pinterest, Bitcoin, Nest home automation, Apple SIRI voice interface, Uber, WeChat, Apple Car Play, Android Auto, Amazon Echo voice interaction, Fitbit wearable device, Apple Watch, Oculus Rift virtual reality	Integrated Information Spaces Information society 2006–Present

Table 2.1 above represents the evolution from a generalist point of view. The pre-history of the web, including Vannevar Bush's Memex (Bush, 1945) and other early ideas around information

spaces and information architecture could fill a book of its own. Similarly, many internet developments along the way are left out, like ALOHAnet (Abramson, 1970), PHP/MySQL Server, and Blogspot. However, the trend is clear that we are on a trajectory from one of limited access by specialists to interaction and connections (almost) everywhere for (almost) everyone.

2.2   FOUNDATION

> *In 1971 a team of engineers drove around Philadelphia night after night in a trailer home stocked with sensitive radio equipment, trying to set up the first working cell phone system* (Gertner, 2012, p. 3).

The foundational generation of the web is when many of the technologies that power the information spaces we take for granted were developed at universities and industrial labs. For the most part these technologies were created by and for researchers and scientists who had a vision of a connected future. The book *Where Wizards Stay Up Late*, by Hafner and Lyon (1998), provides an excellent insight into this time, which has its spirit of invention characterized by their passage on Ray Tomlinson's inclusion of the @ symbol in email addresses:

> *"I got there first, so I got to choose any punctuation I wanted," Tomlinson said, "I chose the @ sign." The character also had the advantage of meaning "at" the designated institution. He had no idea he was creating an icon for the wired world.*

This was a time of experimentation and discovery, mostly out of sight of the general public. The internet grew out of ARPAnet, a network of connected computers initially developed for the military and later turned to the civilian uses of research and education. Access at this point was mostly limited to people at research centers and universities. Most people had little reason, or ability to connect. Developments like the World Wide Web by Tim Berners-Lee at CERN and opening of the internet to a wider audience (S.272 - High-Performance Computing Act of 1991) ushered in the Web1.0 generation.

2.3   WEB1.0

Web1.0 is characterized by public access to the web—when the internet really became a thing that many people could use. Graphical browsers like Netscape Navigator and Internet Explorer provided access to multimedia content, although limited by low-bandwidth modem connections. Dial-up providers like America Online and Compuserve, web search engines like Lycos, and portals like Yahoo! provided access to websites for school, work, and play over telephone lines that had long served homes and businesses. Email, chat rooms, and instant messenger apps handled interpersonal messages. Millions of people adopted the web as a place for learning, communicating, connecting, and entertainment.

Most web pages were static, consisting of text, links, and images (JPG or GIF formats) organized by tables or frames. Little more than hyperlinks connected information resources; users navigated around the web to find what they were looking for. Microsoft Windows remained the main platform for computer use, while the web was supplemental. Very little personalization or customization was possible, although database-backed dynamic content grew in importance.

Many of the technologies and companies we rely on today were first used in this generation, including Google, WiFi, and eCommerce. Demand for increasingly interactive websites, and the technology to support them, ushered in a fast-changing digital landscape. Improvements in bandwidth, user interfaces, and social media soon paved the way for increased interactivity in the web2.0 generation, where information architecture started to become more and more important.

2.4   WEB2.0

While the term "Web2.0" (coined by Tim O'Reilly) has fallen out of use, it marked a turning point in the evolution of the web, setting the stage for today's integrated information spaces. Although many existed beforehand, web2.0 popularized and made central to the online experience several technologies, including:

- mashups;

- personalization and aggregators;

- rich internet applications;

- tagging and hashtags;

- wikis, blogs, and social media; and

- web office applications.

So many of these technologies are ingrained in our experiences that we do not differentiate by name any longer, they are just part of "the web," a constant part of our information experience.

2.4.1   MASHUPS

Mashups allow developers to create apps that support users by combining separate technologies into something new (Merrill, 2006; Yu et al., 2008). A prime example is utilizing Google maps to show locations of restaurants and/or businesses, along with reviews (Figure 2.1). The result looks like a new standalone app, but behind the scenes two or more data sources are combined, or "mashed" together. Web application programming interfaces (APIs) enable sites to share their content for use in mashups.

Behind the scenes, APIs consist of "endpoints" that publish data in a format like JSON or XML for other systems to access and reuse (Rodriguez, 2008). Figure 2.2 shows an example of a result for a query sent to the U.S. National Library of Medicine's MedlinePlus endpoint that returned data in XML format. In the query, we asked the API to return results for the term "diabetes" from their Health Topics database. You can try it yourself by following instructions at https://medlineplus.gov/webservices.html.

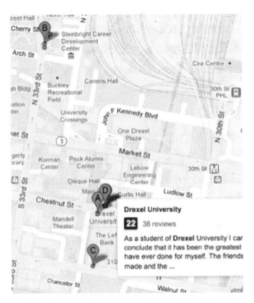

Figure 2.1: A maps mashup combining search, geographic, and reviews data sources.

```
- <nlmSearchResult>
    <term>"diabetes</term>
    <file>viv_OiMRJo</file>
    <server>pvlbsrch16</server>
    <count>260</count>
    <retstart>0</retstart>
    <retmax>10</retmax>
  - <list num="260" start="0" per="10">
    - <document rank="2" url="https://medlineplus.gov/diabetes.html">
        <content name="title"><span class="qt0">Diabetes</span></content>
        <content name="organizationName">National Library of Medicine</content>
        <content name="altTitle"><span class="qt0">Diabetes Mellitus</span></content>
        <content name="altTitle">Sugar <span class="qt0">Diabetes</span></content>
        <content name="altTitle">DM</content>
      - <content name="FullSummary">
          <p><span class="qt0">Diabetes</span> is a disease in which your blood glucose, or blood sugar, levels are too high.
          Glucose comes from the foods you eat. Insulin is a hormone that helps the glucose get into your cells to give them energy.
          With type 1 <span class="qt0">diabetes</span>, your body does not make insulin. With type 2 <span
          class="qt0">diabetes</span>, the more common type, your body does not make or use insulin well. Without enough insulin,
          the glucose stays in your blood. You can also have prediabetes. This means that your blood sugar is higher than normal but
          not high enough to be called <span class="qt0">diabetes</span>. Having prediabetes puts you at a higher risk of getting type
          2 <span class="qt0">diabetes</span>.</p><p>Over time, having too much glucose in your blood can cause serious
          problems. It can damage your eyes, kidneys, and nerves. <span class="qt0">Diabetes</span> can also cause heart disease,
          stroke and even the need to remove a limb. Pregnant women can also get <span class="qt0">diabetes</span>, called
          gestational <span class="qt0">diabetes</span>.</p><p>Blood tests can show if you have <span
          class="qt0">diabetes</span>. One type of test, the A1C, can also check on how you are managing your <span
          class="qt0">diabetes</span>. Exercise, weight control and sticking to your meal plan can help control your <span
          class="qt0">diabetes</span>. You should also monitor your blood glucose level and take medicine if prescribed.
          </p><p>NIH: National Institute of <span class="qt0">Diabetes</span> and Digestive and Kidney Diseases</p>
        </content>
        <content name="mesh"><span class="qt0">Diabetes Mellitus</span></content>
        <content name="groupName">Seniors</content>
        <content name="groupName">Endocrine System</content>
        <content name="groupName">Metabolic Problems</content>
        <content name="groupName"><span class="qt0">Diabetes Mellitus</span></content>
      - <content name="snippet">
```

Figure 2.2: **Results in XML format for the API query,** https://wsearch.nlm.nih.gov/ws/query?d-b=healthTopics&term=%22diabetes.

2.4.2   PERSONALIZATION AND AGGREGATION

Many sites in the web2.0 generation allowed users to remix and control data that appeared on websites they visited. Users could manually subscribe to news feeds and blogs, add tools or services, and link applications and arrange them in a meaningful way for personal use. On banking websites, for example, users could add their credit cards and billing information, or track investments from different resources. Example of aggregation websites from this generation include: Netvibes, Pageflakes, iGoogle, and Yahoo!

Corporate intranet sites, in particular, were places where customization and personalization became popular. For example, at a large university the intranet could include course registrations, course materials, financial aid, payroll, and many others. Depending on the user type (student, faculty, staff) different information was available to each user type. Individual users were able to customize and select components, and include news and events or other university content on their homepage. In addition to the explicit customization described above, some sites also implemented implicit personalization—tailoring the website content based on a user's profile or activity. A good example of this was Amazon.com's ability to recommend new items based on past purchases at their eCommerce site.

2.4.3   RICH INTERNET APPS

Rich Internet Apps (RIA) provided methods for users to interact with information over the web (Fraternali et al., 2010). Although the term has fallen out of favor, RIA features are included in many websites and apps today. Imagine trying to use apps without these features:

- direct manipulation (e.g., drag and drop to move objects/components around on the page);

- immediate system feedback/messaging for error handling or contextual help;

- typeahead text predictions;

- mouseover objects to show additional information;

- automatic saving of user-entered information; and

- refreshing information on parts of a web page without having to reload the entire page.

2.4.4   TAGGING AND HASHTAGS

Tagging gives users the power to label and categorize resources using freely chosen keywords. Compare this to a traditional library, where a professional cataloger assigns a resource into a previously defined category, even when that resource does not fit neatly or addresses several topics. Tags are especially important for categorizing with user-centered, emerging, and event-based keywords, which may not yet (or ever) be in a controlled vocabulary—and in spaces like Twitter where there is no central cataloging authority. IAs can leverage this framework of unstructured tags contributed by users to provide additional access points. Golder and Huberman (2006) found that the application of tags follows predictable patterns; and other researchers found tags themselves can be categorized, such as personalized tags like "toread" (Marlow et al., 2006).

Tags have evolved in many systems to "hashtags," which are labels preceded by the hash or pound symbol "#." Much like the "@" symbol has been coopted by email, the hash symbol is now associated with tags. For example, the hashtag "#PhillyCHI" on Twitter provides access to any tweet a user chose to categorize as related to the Philadelphia chapter of the ACM SIGCHI. Many sites and apps allow users to assign hashtags to information resources. Examples of information spaces that leverage tagging include Pinterest, Flickr, Twitter, and Instagram (see for example, the Instagram post in Figure 2.3).

Figure 2.3: An image posted by Drexel University to Instagram, with hashtags for related topics (libraryscience, etc).

2.4.5   WIKIS, BLOGS, AND SOCIAL MEDIA

Compared with other web2.0 applications, wikis and blogs (although they existed during the web1.0 era) were more user driven. Wikis and blogs are platforms for individuals to easily express themselves, share ideas with other people, get feedback, and contribute to the public knowledge base in a very dynamic manner. While wikis adopted a democratic model for people to freely collaborate on shared topics of interest (e.g. Wikipedia), blogs allowed authors (bloggers) to self-publish articles and other materials. Company blogs became a creative way for the business to engage and communicate with their customers in a more casual environment. Blog and wikis gave anyone with a connection the ability to contribute their thoughts, ideas, and creativity to the web. Table 2.2 shares some examples of public wikis and blogs. In the corporate enterprise, companies like IBM also researched these tools (and other social media) for use in behind the firewall, available only to company employees (DiMicco et al., 2008).

Table 2.2: Examples of wikis and blogs	
Wiki	**Blogging**
Wikipedia	Blogger
Wikitravel	Tumblr
Wikibooks	Wordpress

Social media helps people connect, share, and keep in touch with close friends and family and a wider range of acquaintances. Examples of social media sites include Facebook, Twitter, Flickr, and LinkedIn. Users can post updates and information including text, images, and video—while also reading and reacting to their network's activities. Social media sites are used for general networking like Facebook and Twitter, for topic-specific activities like Flickr (photography) or LinkedIn (business connections). There are even social networks for people with similar medical conditions, such as PatientsLikeMe, where users can share information on treatments and emotional support.

2.4.6   WEB OFFICE APPLICATIONS

Web office apps provided word processing, spreadsheets, and other productivity software through a web browser. This connected experience gave users the ability to work on a single document stored online with multiple devices. Office 365 and Google docs are popular examples of web office apps today. Collaboration emerged as a prime benefit, several authors could edit a single document instead of emailing copies back and forth. Web office apps helped to pave the way for cloud applications, and the growth of the Software as a Service (SaaS) industry.

2.5   INTEGRATED GENERATION

Building on the web2.0 era, technologies in the integrated era are generally liberated from a specific device or location. Where at the web's release a computer with a wired connection was required, Wifi and wireless (cellular) networks today provide a connection in most of the developed and much of the developing world. Mobile continues to grow; a 2016 report by the Pew Research Center finds 72% of people in the U.S. own a smartphones (including over 90% of those aged 18–34); while South Korea leads the surveyed countries, where a reported 88% of the population (and a remarkable 100% of 18–34 year olds) own a smartphone (Poushter, 2016).

Even automotive companies are in on the act; below is some copy from Chevrolet advertising the WiFi features of their cars:

Our stronger signal means you have a fast and reliable connection. Stream movies and TV on the go, or even play games. And so you know, the built-in WiFi hot spot is powered by your vehicle, so you don't have to worry about your mobile device battery. That way, you can keep the action going (Chevrolet, n.d.).

In short, many people are almost always within arm's reach of a device with a web connection, ready to search or create new information, connect with friends and colleagues, or be entertained. Sensors and wearables connect and provide information even without explicit interaction. Given the demographic trends, expect that all types of connectivity will continue to grow in both developed and developing countries, for all sorts of technologies (Figure 2.4).

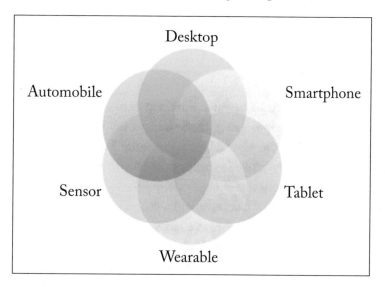

Figure 2.4: Integrated information spaces.

The integrated era is characterized by technologies and concepts, such as:

- artificial intelligence/automated assistants;

- cloud;

- mobile;

- sensors and the internet of things;

- wearables; and

- ubiquity and user-centered design.

2.5.1   ARTIFICIAL INTELLIGENCE, AUTOMATED ASSISTANTS

Now that we live in a world of information overload, technology is helping us sort through the noise to find what we want. The ever growing landscape of technologies leads to the need for ever "smarter" assistants or agents (Maes, 1994). Examples of popular assistants that utilize artificial intelligence (AI) include: Siri (Apple), Alexa (Amazon), Google Assistant, Cortana (Microsoft), and Watson (IBM).

Assistants are intended to appear "smart." They rely on machine learning and artificial intelligence to efficiently complete routine tasks, and provide answers the user may not be able to find on their own. In fields like medicine, IBM's Watson provides answers for doctors who input symptoms; while in the home assistants can help automate tasks, share reminders, and help other aspects of day-to-day life.

2.5.2   CLOUD

Cloud computing provides two major benefits. First, access to large amounts of storage and second, access to powerful computer-processing hardware over the internet. Web office apps, games, and others all take advantage of these capabilities. The entire SaaS industry, for example, is built to provide business services "in the cloud" to millions or billions of users. As software and storage is no longer limited to a user's device, new opportunities for collaboration open up. Additionally, startups can leverage "enterprise class" hardware, without great up-front costs, opening the door for entrepreneurs to launch innovative businesses at a large scale.

Big tech companies like SAP, IBM, and others have as a key part of their strategy moving their services from an installed base, requiring a client to purchase or lease many servers and copies of individual software, to "the cloud." Cloud also means updates can be "pushed" to clients without the need to install anything new. Google docs and Zoho paved the path toward the wide acceptance of online productivity apps, and now almost any task can be completed "online." Major cloud providers include: Amazon AWS, Microsoft Axure, and Google Cloud.

2.5.3   MOBILE

Mobile devices are almost everywhere today, making it hard to believe that they are a relatively new invention. Beginning with the release of the iPhone in 2007 (although devices like Blackberry preceded it), smartphones became mainstream devices. Supported by cellular data, mobile devices took off quickly and now account for a large percentage of user's "screen time." In fact, many people reach for a smartphone even when a more "capable" device like a laptop computer is nearby. Mobile opened up a whole new world of interactions for IAs to explore, including components like GPS and cameras, apps able to leverage those components in new ways, and as an always on device they support push notifications and event-based interactions. Because mobile devices are not typically shared, they support personalization and customization based on the user's preference.

2.5.4   SENSORS AND THE INTERNET OF THINGS

Perhaps the best experience with information spaces is one in which the technology seems to "disappear" (Weiser, 1991). In addition to systems supporting information creation and consumption by human users, sensors and "the internet of things" opens a new world of "invisible information architecture" by connecting items like automobiles, home thermostats, and even refrigerators to the web. One day (soon?) a refrigerator will tell the user they need milk, or even automatically order it to be delivered by an Uber driver at a time the user is home to accept delivery, based on the user's calendar (accessed as a web service mashup). Of course, with drones even the Uber driver may one day be unnecessary.

2.5.5   WEARABLES

Wearables, like Fitbits and Apple watches, generally need to connect with another device like an iPhone to perform all their functions. Sometimes they are used to collect biometric data, like heart rate, and are now advanced to a point where text messages and alerts can appear. While the future appears bright for these devices, from an IA standpoint they tend to be extensions of other devices and apps for the time being. However, they are now part of the information landscape and should be considered in projects as an opportunity to expand IA. In the future they may be decoupled from other devices.

2.5.6   UBIQUITY AND USER-CENTERED DESIGN

In developed countries today there is an expectation that people are connected. Tax forms and other government documents are online. Banking and essential services are conducted through online apps. On a college campus, students search for resources on a library website and download them instantly. For most technology users it is probably more common for a device to be connected than not, providing opportunities for IAs to leverage the capabilities brought about by broadband, cloud, and other technologies. IAs help information spaces work for people by adopting a user-centered approach. This means the users' goals and needs are researched and balanced against the desires of a business or technology limitations. The aim is to make sure people can effectively use the system, and have a good experience. The next chapter covers IA and user-centered design in depth.

In the integrated era, information systems are everywhere—from the home to office and anywhere in-between. Televisions, kitchen appliances, and even Bluetooth-connected showerheads have gotten in on the act. By designing for the information behaviors, user interactions, and adopting the design patterns and principles which we discuss in later chapters, IAs can help mitigate information overload and produce readily learnable interfaces.

Table 2.3: Three generations of the web

	Web1.0	Web2.0	Integrated
Purpose and Motivation	Web presence and eCommerce	User participation (e.g., wikis, blogs); harness collective intelligence	Connect data contextually and semantically; access anytime, anywhere; connect, create, and share
Platform	Windows is the platform; web is supplemental	Web is the "platform"	Information society
Major Ways of Information Access	Web directories (e.g. the original Yahoo!) and earlier search engines (e.g. Lycos, InfoSeek, and AltaVista)	Search engine with popularity-based ranking (e.g., Google); aggregators	Context-sensitive and personalized; data decoupled from device, linked data over the semantic web
Personalization Customization	On individual sites	User-controlled customization across sites, e.g., site aggregators	Context-sensitive personalization and customization
Information Architecture	From less structured links to structure provided by the site owner	Emergent IA based on user activities/ participation	Integration of displays, devices, content structure, linked data, and usage data
Navigation	In-line links, frames pre-determined navigation	Dynamic navigation based on participation	Context-based browsing and links
Look and Feel	Text heavy with some graphics, frames, and tables	Consistent look and feel; branding design; user experience design	Responsive design and interactive interfaces; voice and automated assistants
Web and Apps	Page-based application	Server-driven web applications and pre-compiled web applications	Linked web and mobile apps perform many essential functions in society

Content and Interaction	From static content to database-backed dynamic content	RIAs without page refreshing	Distributed linked data; second screen, user journeys over time and across devices
Modalities and Media Types	From text only to multi-media	Multi-modalities and channels aggregated by the web	Video, mobile, information overload
User Activities	Multiple sites via directories, portals, or search engines; information seeking	User contributing content and tags; communities based on common interests	Participation in the information society

2.6   SUMMARY

Users can create, consume, and connect at ever increasing rates in our integrated era (Table 2.3). Underpinning these advances are previous generations of the web (see Table 2.1) that laid the groundwork for today's information society. Technology predictions are notoriously unreliable, but current trends point toward artificial intelligence and automated systems becoming more integrated into the digital landscape.

Information technology is an industry of constant change and disruption. We included a history of the generations of the web because we feel it is important to look back and understand that human beings invented all the technologies we take for granted, and today we build on what has come before. Information architects will have a large hand in "inventing the future," and should learn to adapt and leverage the right technologies in the right contexts, while also keeping an eye toward creating the new and unexpected.

CHAPTER 3

IA and User-centered Design

Information architects (IAs) are helping to create a "user-centered" future, where user goals and needs serve as the guidelines for design and development. User-centered design (UCD) is the most prevailing methodology for information architecture design. Although some might call it "customer-center design" (Duyne et al., 2002) or "contextual design" (Beyer and Holtzblatt, 1997), the ideas are the same; the "user" should be the center of focus during the whole design process. IAs, and everyone building an information space, must help identify user needs and balance them with business and technical concerns, in order to improve usability and maximize the usefulness of an information space (Figure 3.1). In this chapter, the UCD process for information architecture is introduced.

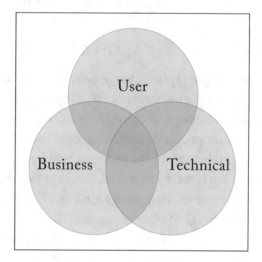

Figure 3.1: User-centered design components: IAs should look to balance user needs with technical limitations and business goals.

3.1 UCD BACKGROUND

UCD is based on domains like human factors and usability and includes elements from the design, computer science, and the psychology fields (Myers, 1998; Sauro, 2013). In fact, UCD is so significant that the International Organization for Standardization (ISO) created several sections on its concepts as they relate to information spaces in ISO 9241. This standard defines important shared concepts for UCD.

With all this focus on users, do we really have an understanding of who they are? Users can be customers or workers, current users or potential users, public users or internal users, experts or novices, early adopters or technophobes… we think you get the point. Human users are multi-faceted and change over time. A novice user can become an expert, or a person can be happy one moment and angry the next. Part of the design process is identifying and prioritizing users as personas (Cooper, 2004; Pruitt and Grudin, 2003), to humanize this concept of users, and coming up with creative solutions that serve their needs.

> User defined: A human being interacting with information space(s) to achieve a goal, in the context of work, information seeking or creating, entertainment, or play. They may be experts or novices, experienced or inexperienced, motivated or disinterested. Like all humans, they will have a range of cognitive, psychological, and physical abilities and limitations, and will have moods and preferences that vary over time.

3.2   INCLUDE USERS IN RESEARCH AND DESIGN

While in the past the user was too often ignored, today gathering user input early and often is considered best practice. Including users in development helps improve everything from websites and software, to car dashboards and automated teller machines (ATMs). For example, BMW's iDrive system for many years landed their cars on a do-not-recommend list, not because of the engine performance or handling, but instead because of the poor user interface for controlling the radio and other features. Today that interface is greatly improved, thanks to user research (Norman, 2002).

The UCD process emphasizes research, design, and evaluation as three iterative activities that should be embedded in every stage of IA development (Figure 3.2). Design and development frameworks, like design sprints (http://www.gv.com/sprint/) or design thinking (Plattner et al., 2016) grounded in UCD concepts are often used to organize the work of interdisciplinary teams, helping to maintain a strong focus on user-centered outcomes.

The human user is easily overlooked when designing information spaces. Many stakeholders (such as business sponsors, programmer/developers, and designers) think, "we know our users, we know what they want" or they listen to the loudest, but not most representative users ("the squeaky wheel gets the grease" syndrome). In our experience, this leads to unnecessary rework fixing problems that should have been identified in the early design phase of a project, substandard systems released for use, the need for expensive follow-up customer care, and unhappy users. UCD goes a long way toward avoiding these issues and has been adopted by organizations that see it as a way to build systems with increased acceptance by consumers and return on investment (Ross, 2014; Whitten et al., 2004).

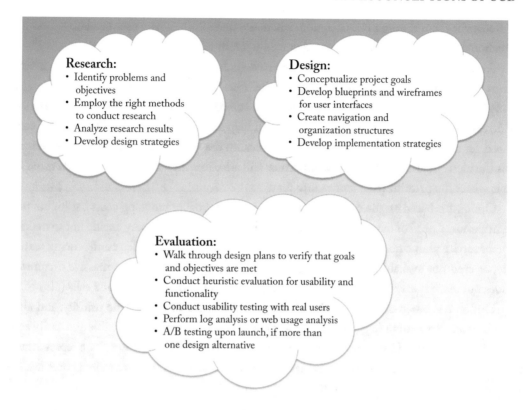

Research:
- Identify problems and objectives
- Employ the right methods to conduct research
- Analyze research results
- Develop design strategies

Design:
- Conceptualize project goals
- Develop blueprints and wireframes for user interfaces
- Create navigation and organization structures
- Develop implementation strategies

Evaluation:
- Walk through design plans to verify that goals and objectives are met
- Conduct heuristic evaluation for usability and functionality
- Conduct usability testing with real users
- Perform log analysis or web usage analysis
- A/B testing upon launch, if more than one design alternative

Figure 3.2: Three clouds of the IA process.

UCD puts the user in the center. However, it does not minimize the influence of other stakeholders. IAs, due to their unique position as researchers and designers, often serve as the "voice of the user" in an organization, and lead UCD processes. We will discuss ISO 9241 and usability from a user standpoint along with a general UCD process in this chapter. In later chapters we will dive into research, design, and evaluation. Before we do that, we need some discussions to clarify potential misconceptions about UCD.

3.3   MISCONCEPTIONS OF UCD

3.3.1   UCD DOES NOT MEAN FOCUSING ONLY ON USER NEEDS AND IGNORING BUSINESS GOALS AND MARKET OPPORTUNITIES

Rather, UCD means that the user is given a voice in the design process, providing IAs and other stakeholders the information they need to make well-informed decisions and align business goals with user needs. How do you resolve a conflict between the user needs, business goals, and technology? Reconcile them through prioritization, where the tradeoffs between user needs, business goals, and technology limitations are known and agreed upon in advance.

For example, suppose that one of the business goals is to reduce the cost of customer service (such as phone calls to a call center), whereas the users' priority is to have help available at any time. What are the implications for the design of a company website? The direct implication is to provide easy-to-use, easy-to-understand, contextual help and a comprehensive Help Center so that the need for calling the company is minimized, because the website answers most user questions. This is the ideal situation, but some scenarios may still arise in which the user needs even more help. Here is where the prioritization comes into play.

Option 1 is based on the conclusion that the business goal of reducing costs has higher priority than the users' need of having help easily available. Therefore, the IA may decide not to make any customer service phone number (or instant messaging, click to chat, or video conferencing features) visible, or even not available to the user at all. For example Amazon.com, a massive e-commerce site does not make it easy to contact customer service for real-time chat or phone calls (Figure 3.3).

Option 2 is based on the opposite conclusion, that the user need is the priority, and always having contact information (e.g., phone number, click to call or chat) highly visible and easily accessible is the right design. However, this may increase the need for more customer care representatives to handle an increase in direct calls or contact. Because this solution requires more people available to answer phone calls, it can increase the business costs.

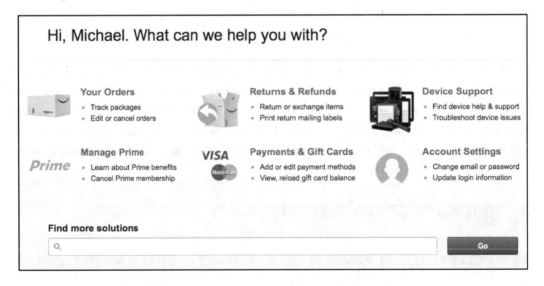

Figure 3.3: Help section on Amazon.com with categories and no easy "contact us" option—but links to answer common questions.

Which one is the right choice? It really depends on the situation. Depending on the business model, company culture, and other factors, some companies (e.g., financial companies) are more likely to think direct contact increases opportunities to earn more business from users; so making it easy to call the company wins here. Other companies may deem cutting costs for customer support as the first business priority, so keeping phone numbers and chat off the site wins in this case. There is not a right or wrong answer that will satisfy everyone in every situation. It is part of the IA's role to balance competing factors to help the team prioritize.

3.3.2   UCD DOES NOT MEAN THAT THE DESIGN IS AGAINST INTRODUCING NEW TECHNOLOGIES OR CHANGES

Technology-centered design, where technical concerns trump others, is like preparing a meal by equipping the kitchen with utensils and then ignoring quality of ingredients. You may have the most advanced kitchen possible, but nobody will want to eat the food you prepare. New technologies must be incorporated intelligently, while serving a purpose, not just for their own sake. Without a thorough understanding of users, it is hard for design to provide value to the user and the business while introducing new technology. At the same time, it is critical for design professionals to be sensitive to the capabilities of newly available technologies and leverage them to improve the user experience and design.

Sometimes certain technology may change the way people interact with a system, and managing changes is always a challenge for IAs. For example, new interactive features on websites may promise to improve the user experience by making the interaction more efficient, direct, and less cumbersome. Although it may take time for the user to get used to new interactions, designers should consider creating suitable paths for the user to overcome initial barriers and increase usability in the long term. The key is to find the best match between problems at hand and the right technology, balancing features and learnability.

3.3.3   UCD DOES NOT MEAN THAT USERS THEMSELVES CAN BEST DESIGN FOR THEIR OWN USE

UCD is really about the design driven by user needs. Users are usually very good at telling what problems they have; they do not necessarily always have good solutions. A famous quote has been attributed to Henry Ford: "If I would have asked my customers what they wanted, they would have asked for a faster horse." This means that while users may be able to identify problems they face, they do not always have the expertise, experience, or creativity to come up with innovative solutions that may solve those problems.

In general, it is the designer's and the IA's responsibility to clearly understand user problems and user needs, and transform them into robust design solutions. One might remember the classic episode of The Simpsons, where Homer meets his long lost brother, gets to design his dream car (while ignoring professional designers), and eventually ruins his brother's business (George, 2014). That story tells us what might happen when users try to design for themselves.

3.4   ISO 9241

Up to this point, we have discussed how UCD includes users in the design and development process, and how to balance user needs with other priorities. But how does an IA put these ideas into practice? Fortunately, the concepts behind UCD are codified by ISO, the International Organization for Standardization, in "ISO 9241: Ergonomics of human-system interaction" (2010). The standard, which supersedes ISO 13407, describes concepts, hardware design, software design, and the design processes related to UCD. ISO 9241 defines several important terms for IA, including a useful and concise definition of *usability*.

3.4.1   USABILITY

Usability is the core concept when designing for users. ISO 9241 defines usability as the "extent to which a product can be used by specified users to achieve specified goals with effectiveness, efficiency and satisfaction in a specified context of use." In order to make "usability" actionable and measurable, let's examine the three components and ISO's definitions of each (ISO, 1998).

1. **Effectiveness:** Accuracy and completeness with which users achieve specified goals.

2. **Efficiency:** Resources expended in relation to the accuracy and completeness with which users achieve goals.

3. **Satisfaction:** Freedom from discomfort, and positive attitudes toward the use of the product.

Effectiveness, efficiency, and satisfaction can all be measured in meaningful ways, helping IAs understand if a system is meeting user needs and goals, or if improvement is needed. Quantitative statistics on usability (Sauro and Lewis, 2016), combined with qualitative feedback like interviews and comments, let the IA paint a full picture of usability. Examples of data collected to measure usability include:

- **Effectiveness:** Task completion rates/errors;

- **Efficiency:** Time on task; and

- **Satisfaction:** User ratings.

Measuring usability is applicable to many types of systems, including software applications, websites, consumer apps, games, and medical devices. Importantly, improving effectiveness, efficiency, and satisfaction gives IAs targets to work toward and success metrics to evaluate their work.

Let's apply concepts from ISO 9241 in an example from industry, to show how usability can have a real-world impact. Imagine a large software enterprise with tens of thousands of employees who often have to find information on a company intranet. Employees complain that finding information is difficult and takes a lot of time, and managers notice that even the top performing teams are sometimes not prepared. An exploratory investigation of the intranet shows that employees often take several hours to find information critical to their jobs. Clearly, the information is not easily accessible. However, the company faces stiff competition and needs to improve the products that it sells. Organizing information and making the intranet more usable seems to be a poor allocation of the company's IA efforts, which could be used to create better selling software products. The employees just have to "get better" at finding things, right?

In fact, if we consider ISO's effectiveness and efficiency, balancing the usability of the intranet against other priorities becomes easy. Estimating that an improved intranet can save one hour per week per employee by helping them find what they need faster (increasing efficiency), we can judge the benefits the company will see versus the cost to redesign. Measuring the average time it takes to find documents before, and comparing it to the time it takes afterward shows the impact of the work—and when employees are more efficient the company saves money. To go further, we could look at the effectiveness of the intranet. What happens if a salesperson cannot find important documents that will help her close the sale, or a software developer cannot find documentation that explains how a system works and writes code that has a lot of bugs? What would the loss to the company be then? And all of this has not even touched on satisfaction yet. Happy employees are generally productive employees.

Taken together, a redesign of the intranet may be a great business decision due to improved productivity. By applying the concepts of effectiveness, efficiency, and satisfaction the benefits become clear. In fact, some organizations even go so far as to mandate internal systems must be redesigned if they score below a certain threshold on a widely accepted usability scale, in order to help maintain a high level of employee productivity.

3.5   UCD DESIGN PROCESS

UCD includes design of things the user sees (front end, user interface) and design of things the user will never see (behind the scenes, back end). Think about it like a car, the engine is almost never seen but has a huge impact on performance, while the steering wheel is always seen and has the biggest impact on user control of the direction. Figure 3.4 illustrates a UCD design process for information architecture. There are two parallel processes in design:

1. the front-end UI design, and

2. the behind the scenes metadata and controlled vocabulary design.

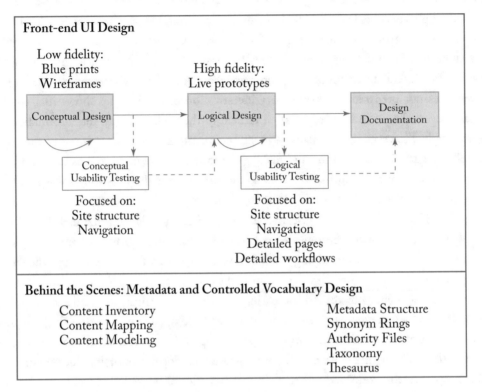

Figure 3.4: Detailed view of the design process with two parallel process, front end and behind the scenes.

In most cases, the two should go hand in hand. For example, when designing a search capability, the UI piece looks fairly simple (search box, results display), but the majority of the work is behind the scenes in metadata and content. Without appropriate metadata schema, search engine indexing, keywords, relevance ranking mechanism, or controlled vocabulary, search could easily fail. This parallel work is very visible in a faceted search interface (Hearst, 2009; Tunkelang, 2009), where metadata is placed directly in the UI as filters which the user can apply to limit their search results to specific terms.

3.5.1   FRONT END UI DESIGN

While information architects and content people do most of the work behind the scenes, the upfront UI design involves IAs along with visual designers, user/usability researchers, and others.

Although the UI design constantly evolves and iterates, it is still meaningful to differentiate the high-level conceptual design from the more detailed logical design. The beginning conceptual design is more focused on the site structure and navigation—whether the user can easily tell where they are or what they can do, whether the labels make sense, and where else they can go from here. Visual details and specific interactions are handled during logical design—which is closer to the final look of the interface users will see.

Usability tests are recommended at the end of each sub-phase to examine the design with a sample of targeted users. The feedback is then incorporated into the iteration. Appropriate usability tests may be conducted before and during each design phase. The key is to test early so that problems can be identified and fixed more easily and less expensively than finding them later. Tests may include an entire interface, or just a specific feature or function. Finding the correct users to test with is very important; they must match the characteristics of the projected users for the final product.

A note on roles: information architects, user experience designers, user experience researchers, interaction designers, visual designers, (and more!) all have an important role to play in creating usable interfaces. However, a single person may take on one or more roles, like filling both the IA and UX designer roles. To make things even more confusing, there is no standardization in the names of roles across the industry (yes, that's right—the people tasked with creating labels and organization have not standardized their own terminology). Generally speaking, larger projects will have a single person dedicated to each role, while on smaller projects people will hold more than one role, and may even be a "team of one."

3.5.2   BEHIND THE SCENES: METADATA AND CONTROLLED VOCABULARY DESIGN

Information architects and content people work behind the scenes developing content and its related metadata and taxonomy. This work is often performed in parallel with UI design. Here, we see the dual roles IAs can play—designing the front end and working the behind the scenes as well. On small or medium projects this helps increase efficiency because the IA has knowledge of both. On larger projects, it may not be possible for one IA to work on both the front end and behind the scenes. In these cases, knowledge transfer is needed to ensure the efforts are aligned, making teamwork and communication an important part of effective IA.

Metadata and taxonomy development directly inform the design of the navigation and have a big impact on the user experience. Methods like content inventories, card sorting, and tree testing can all be used to create and evaluate the behind-the-scenes IA work, with the goal of matching a user's mental models of an information space with the structure created by IAs. This can be quite challenging, and has long been studied in the library sciences. We discuss metadata and taxononmy concepts more fully in Chapter 5.

3.5.3   DESIGN DELIVERABLES

Information architects (along with other experts) create many deliverables during the design phase (shown in Figures 3.5, 3.6, and 3.7), used by the team to develop and communicate designs.

- For conceptual design: blueprints (or high-level IA diagram), wireframe (low-fidelity), work-flow diagrams/story boards.

- For logical design: detailed wire frame and prototype, used for various design reviews and user tests.

- Final documentation: UI specification document, detailed navigation diagram, and detailed IA diagram. They are meant for the developers to fully implement the design.

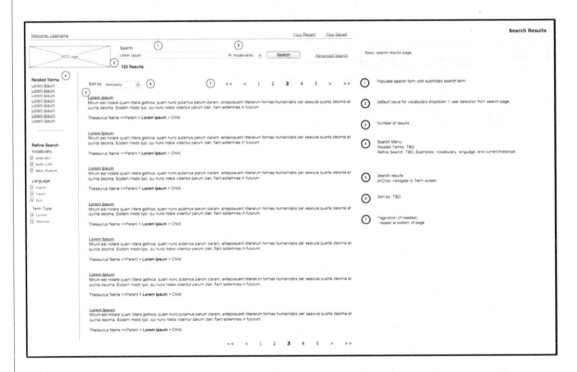

Figure 3.5: Example low-fidelity wireframe showing a search results page. On the right are annotations that describe the functionality called out in the screen (#1, 2, 3, etc.).

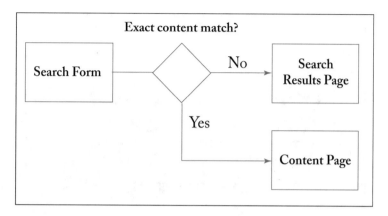

Figure 3.6: Example flow showing the path from a search form. The user goes to a search results page, unless the keyword is an exact content match, in which case the system takes them to the content page.

3.5.4 UCD TEAMS

Creating complex information spaces requires an interdisciplinary team involving business sponsors, user researchers, visual designers, software developers, project managers, content writers, and others. With so many "stakeholders," in order for everyone to collaborate effectively, roles and responsibilities should be made clear. The process may vary from project to project depending on many factors, but the ultimate goal should be the same: increase the business value of the design and meet the user needs. We'll discuss more about teams in a later chapter.

In many organizations, UCD is embedded into the overall system/application development process. While information architects create conceptual designs (sketching design concepts) and other deliverables, product owners and business analysts (BA) gather business and technical requirements. Conceptual designs are often used to guide the requirement-gathering activities, and the requirements in turn help refine the design. In our experience as IAs in technology organizations, the IA and BA work closely together cross-referencing requirements and conceptual designs. Only after business requirements are officially gathered, reviewed, and finalized, can the IT team make realistic commitments to the level of effort needed. In development frameworks like Agile (which we discuss later in the book), requirements are often expressed as "user stories" and kept in a prioritized backlog for the team to develop incrementally.

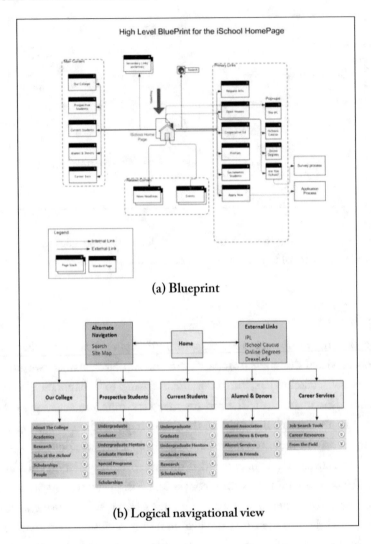

(a) Blueprint

(b) Logical navigational view

Figure 3.7: Examples of IA deliverables, blueprint, and logical navigation (courtesy of Stephen Croce (a) and Ryan Phillips (b)).

- User Story Format: "As a user, I want to _____, so that I can _____."

- "As a library science graduate student, I want to filter library search results, so that I can see only peer-reviewed articles."

Having official business requirements will greatly benefit the design work. The following defines what the requirements will do:

- Ensure that the system's expected behavior is captured, documented, and understood by both the business client and the IT project team.

- Define boundaries of the system, what is in scope and what is out of scope.

- Provide basis for more precise estimation of costs and schedule.

- Establish and maintain agreement with business stakeholders on what the systems should do.

Note that many software development methodologies used in industry place a premium on working features over written documentation describing the feature. Thus the relationship between IA and software development is evolving, and each organization has its own flavor of collaboration. Some teams are reducing the amount of written or static documentation and instead substituting working prototypes created by the IA, using software to produce interactive interfaces. There is no single "best" solution, so it is important to choose methods that most effectively communicate with others on the team, and help improve efficiency.

3.5.5   ITERATIVE DESIGN

"I have not failed. I've just found 10,000 ways that won't work." —Thomas Edison

Iterative design is based on the notion that "it is unlikely that the first implementation of any user interface is going to function as well as it could or should" and you should "keep trying until you get it right" (Buxton and Sniderman, 1980). The iterative design process is a core principle of ISO 9241. While Figure 3.4 shows the design process in a linear fashion, in reality the IA may revisit conceptual design and logical design several times, while working toward the optimum design. Buxton and Sniderman (1980) and Nielsen (1993) described iterative computer interface design as a process of prototyping, testing, evaluating results, and refining. Incremental improvements of a single, improving interface toward a state of completion are the goal.

3.5.6   ITERATIVE DESIGN FRAMEWORKS

Iterative design has recently been widely embraced by the IA and startup communities. Translating ideas into practice led to the development of frameworks that help organizations structure their work, and incorporate regular user feedback into their deliverables. The fundamentals remain since Buxton, Sniderman, Nielsen, and others described them: You are unlikely to get it right the first time, test with users to see what is not working, fix what does not work, and test again. These frameworks make iterative design accessible to programmers, business owners, and others who do not have training in IA.

GV Design Sprints

As an example of iterative design in the modern enterprise, let's look at design sprints. Google Ventures (now officially GV, a part of Alphabet, Inc.) developed a five-day "design sprint" to quickly build and test prototypes with "real live humans" (http://www.gv.com/sprint). Design sprints are meant to quickly launch a Minimum Viable Product (MVP) that has the minimum features required, and gather user feedback for improvements, before committing to costly development. GV describes it as a "shortcut to learning." The five-day sprint process is as follows.

- **Monday:** Collect knowledge from others in the organization, develop a shared understanding of the problem, and agree on the problem to be solved.

- **Tuesday:** Review what's been tried before, develop new ideas, and start recruiting participants for a Friday usability test.

- **Wednesday:** Decide which single idea (Tuesday) to test, create prototype designs. Schedule participants for the Friday test, and start creating the test plan.

- **Thursday:** Develop a testable prototype (may require a programmer's help) and finalize test planning.

- **Friday:** Conduct a usability test, analyze the results, and plan next steps.

In practice, sprints do not always need to follow the exact format as GV—but the spirit remains the same. Design sprints are all about doing the minimum of work to gain the most knowledge about usability and where to take the design next. By limiting the cycle to just a few days, the goal is that progress is consistent and little work is wasted. Even in the unlikely event a design totally fails, only a week is lost, an idea known as "fail fast." Fail fast beats working on a project for a year, hoping you got it right only to learn that it was wrong.

3.6   SUMMARY

User-centered design is a methodology that includes users in the process, where their needs guide design and development, while balancing business and technical requirements. IAs often lead UCD efforts while serving as the "voice of the user." Iterative design, combining research, design, and evaluation is the best way to produce user-centered products, as it is almost impossible to get it right the first time.

ISO 9241 provides a foundation for UCD, including definitions for the terms usability, effectiveness, efficiency, and satisfaction. In the following chapters, we will explore the standard's specification for four user-centered design activities (ISO, 2010):

- understand and specify the context of use;

- specify user requirements;

- produce design solutions to meet these requirements; and

- evaluate the designs against requirements .

The four activities seem so easy, and common sense. Yet, again and again, steps are skipped or user requirements are ignored, leading to systems with poor usability, or even systems that are totally abandoned. In an iterative design environment, learning and understanding are built into the process, and IAs design systems with the user in mind, helping to ensure products meet target user needs.

CHAPTER   4

IA Research and Evaluation

Information architecture research and evaluation provides the foundation for creating user-centered information spaces. Research and evaluation go together; we start learning through *research* about users' goals and needs, *design and build* in an attempt to meet those needs, and then *evaluate* to see how well what we built performs. Research helps to *build the right thing*—the features and tools that users want, and evaluation helps make sure we *build the thing right*—that the thing performs as intended (Hanson, 2013), where the "thing" is an information system.

In this chapter we discuss user research and evaluation methods in the context of continuous improvement and iterative design. Notice in Figure 4.1 that research and evaluation are next to one another when thinking in terms of iterative cycles. While we show distinct boxes here, in practice the areas tend to blend into one another. We think about it like this: Research is learning about user goals and needs, while evaluation is helping to determine how well a design meets those goals and needs. Research and evaluation are sometimes given the labels "generative research" and "evaluative research" in practice.

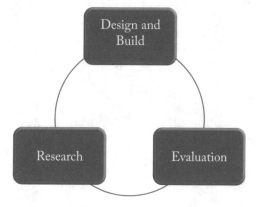

Figure 4.1: An iterative research-to-evaluation process.

4.1   RESEARCH

Any design process requires significant research activities in order to learn about users and how to meet their needs. For information architecture, research does the following:

- collects objective data from users to learn behavior and context;

- collects relevant facts, best practices, and design principles that help the team formulate and understand an overall design strategy;

- lays the foundation for IA strategy and design work; and

- saves time and avoids unnecessary mistakes in design and development parts of the project; increases the chances for successful adoption by users.

4.1.1   RESEARCH METHODS

IA research focuses on context, content, and users. Context research deals mainly with the business and technology elements of UCD teams. It is important that IAs learn about their organization's technology capabilities and business objectives, so they can be matched to user goals and needs. Content and user research methods are focused more on how information is presented and the user element. By conducting content and user research, IAs gather the data essential to designing for user needs. Rosenfeld et al. (2015) provide a good summary of these three research areas. We reproduced their summary in Figure 4.2.

CONTEXT	Background research	Presentations and meetings	Stakeholder interviews	Technology assessment
CONTENT	Heuristic evaluation	Metadata and content analysis	Content mapping	Benchmarking
USERS	Search log and clickstream analysis	Use cases and personas	Contextual inquire	User interviews and user testing

Figure 4.2: Research methods and activities based on Rosenfeld et al., 2015 (p. 315).

While IA is primarily focused on content and user research, it is critical to understand the organization's objectives and team capabilities. Some additional details on the activities above include:

- **Context:** Understand the problems and challenges as well as the business goals and objectives; develop short-term and long-term goals; learn existing technical infrastructure; develop schedules and budgets. Interview and develop working relationships with stakeholders.

- **Content research:** Learn who creates, maintains or updates, and owns content, how content is currently used. Think about competitive benchmarking and before-and-after benchmarking. One of the first activities may be to conduct a study to gather the "before" benchmarking data.

- **User research:** Understand the behaviors, goals and needs, environment and culture, workflows, and sophistication/expertise levels of users.

Outcomes of the IA research methods listed above include:

- clearly stated objectives of the IA project/program;

- one or several research summary reports on users;

- personas, scenarios, navigation structures, and user flows; and

- IA strategy, including recommendations, rationales, and justifications supported by the data.

4.1.2   CONTENT AND USER RESEARCH AND METHODS

A detailed comparison of selected content and user research methods (along with several more not in Figure 4.2) is shared in Table 4.1, with pros and cons as well as appropriate uses. The goal is to help you select the best method for your research purposes. Note that some methods are usually combined together to provide a more comprehensive view of the user and context. For example, very often usability testing and interview methods are combined to understand what happened through observation in the usability test and additional detail through an interview that takes place during the same session.

Research/Evaluation Method	Best Used For ...
	Table 4.1: Comparison of IA content and user research methods
A/B testing	Comparing two or more versions of an interface in order to see which performs better. Often automated through the use of testing software. **Pros:** Can collect quantitative data to see which design performs better against desired metrics in natural user interaction settings, in a non-intrusive manner. **Cons:** Can be difficult to set up, requires specialized software. It may take a long time to get significant results.
Card Sorting (open and closed)	Testing IA structures and studying users' mental models. Open card sorting allows the user to create new categories and terms, in addition to existing. Closed card sorting restricts users to existing categories and terms. Terms used in card sorting can be created based upon results from many other research methods, such as interviews, observations, and log analysis. **Pros:** Powerful tool can be used both qualitatively and quantitatively. **Cons:** Quantitative analysis may need special software. Results need to be presented in a meaningful way.
Competitive Analysis	Assessing the strengths and weaknesses of comparable systems, and looking for gaps or areas for improvement. **Pros:** Provides a look at how a system compares to its peers. **Cons:** May not provide rich qualitative data.
Content Analysis, Mapping, and Inventory	Understanding the current content in a system and its structure. **Pros:** Provides a full view of the content held by a system or organization. **Cons:** Can be time consuming, may ignore context.
Diary Study	Collecting longitudinal user reports that can be used to follow behaviors, goals, and tasks over time. **Pros:** Collects data over an extended period of time, in the user's natural environment. **Cons:** Can be difficult to set up, high drop out rate among participants.

Research/Evaluation Method	Best Used For ...
Desirability Testing (Benedek and Miner, 2002)	Collecting users' positive, negative, and neutral reactions to a system, by having them choose descriptions from a set of terms provided by the researcher. **Pros:** Easy to set up, provides easy-to-understand visuals. **Cons:** May not provide data explaining users' subjective assessments.
Expert Evaluation	Evaluating systems to identify usability issues using expert knowledge and checklists. **Pros:** Usually easy to perform, can provide results quickly. **Cons:** Does not involve real users. May be biased by the reviewer's skills and background.
Focus Groups	Collecting opinions, ideas, and visioning data. Good for high-level starting points and trend data. **Pros:** Like a group interview. Can reach multiple people at the same time. Participants may be inspired by each other and provide more valuable opinions and ideas. **Cons:** Participant opinions may be influenced by others. Out of context of the task.
Heuristic Evaluation	Evaluating an information space to identify usability issues. Trained evaluators inspect a system using a checklist of heuristics, noting usability issues and categorizing them on a severity scale. **Pros:** Can be completed relatively quickly, does not require recruiting participants. Can provide an ordered list of issues and severity ratings. **Cons:** Does not involve real users, and is dependent on the skill and background of the evaluators.
Interviews	Gaining a quick understanding about users' issues, problems, and questions. Interviews can be stand-alone research or can be combined with other methods. Within the project team, IAs can interview stakeholders to understand business objectives. **Pros:** Less ambiguity, can ask follow-up questions to probe unexpected topics or clarify issues. Easy to conduct. **Cons:** Subjective and retrospective (can be difficult to accurately recall past events).

Research/Evaluation Method	Best Used For ...
Observations/Contextual Inquiry	Understanding users' goals and tasks based on real-life behavior in their natural environment; sometimes called "in the wild," field studies, or ethnography. **Pros:** Data gathering takes place in the context of user's work. Data is more concrete, based on in-the-moment experience. Data is more objective and natural. May discover unanticipated issues. **Cons:** Opportunistic, time-consuming, large amount of data, analysis takes time.
Participatory Design	Developing innovative concepts by co-designing with users. Insights are generally gathered in the form of sketches or other low-fidelity designs. **Pros:** A picture is worth a thousand words, helps users translate their ideas into visuals, which may be more expressive. **Cons:** Users may have differing levels of design interest or expressiveness.
Surveys	Collecting preferences and opinions from one or many large groups through written questionnaires. **Pros:** Able to reach many people. **Cons:** Low response rate. Ambiguity in question and/or answer (no clarification). Subjective (self-reporting) and retrospective (subject to error).
Task Analysis	Understanding users' activities and cognitive processes needed to complete tasks. Hierarchical task analysis (HTA) is a common method used to decompose high-level tasks into a hierarchy of sub-tasks. **Pros:** Identifies what tasks should be considered and supported in a design; what works well and what needs improvement in existing flows. **Cons:** Difficult to determine impact of iterative design/development on identified tasks. Can be time consuming.

Research/Evaluation Method	Best Used For …
Tree Testing	Understanding the performance of a navigation system by observing users' click paths to find information. This is like a reverse card sort. **Pros:** Can identify issues with navigation paths. **Cons:** Does not test the usability of the final navigation design (e.g., mega menus, dropdowns).
Usability Testing (in-person and remote)	Identifying design defects in organization, labeling, navigation and user interface details. Usually combined with an interview for clarification and follow-up. Can be conducted in-person or remotely (over the web), and may be moderated or un-moderated (using specialized software). Techniques like "think aloud" and eye-tracking can be used during the test. **Pros:** Rich data both verbal and behavioral. Materials being tested can be low or high fidelity. **Cons:** Lab setting and artificial tasks may decrease the value of the data. May be hard to include a large number of participants, although can be mitigated with remote testing.
Usage Statistics, Log Analysis, Technical/Customer Support records	Identifying usage patterns and finding problems that need research. For example, search log analysis can help leverage user search language to augment a controlled vocabulary, and identify popular queries and even IA problems (when the site navigation is confusing, the user may use search as the last resort). Use technical support/call center logs to identify common user problems. **Pros:** Data is objective and rich. May discover in-depth information about user flows. **Cons:** Sheer volume of data. May need coding or special software to do analysis.

There are many books and resources that look more deeply into research methods than we can cover here. Some we've used with success in the past include: Kelly's (2009) *Methods for Evaluating Interactive Information Retrieval Systems with Users,* which provides a concise review of detailed concepts in research, such as sampling, hypothesis testing, and study design (available from her website: https://ils.unc.edu/~dianek/FnTIR-Press-Kelly.pdf); Sauro and Lewis's *Quantifying the User Experience* (2016) that deeply explores quantitative research in very accessible terms; and Blandford et al.'s *Qualitative HCI Research: Going Behind the Scenes* (2016) as a review of the qualitative side of research.

In order to choose the right research method or combination of methods, one needs to consider a set of criteria—from the sample size of study participants, nature of data required, and purpose of research—to time and resource constraints. Start with the research questions: what is it that you want to learn? Then choose the participants and methods that you think will answer the questions. Finally, consider how you will present the results. There is no perfect research method, so be sure to carefully consider how you will conduct research to answer your research questions.

Qualitative and Quantitative Data

IAs collect two main types of data in their research, quantitative and qualitative. One way to think about quantitative and qualitative is "numbers and words":

- **Quantitative is numbers:** Shows what happened

  Example: Participant B spent 5 min, 30 s to find the correct web page, versus the average of 3 min.

- **Qualitative is words:** Explains why something happened

  Example: Participant B reported the navigation is "cluttered and confusing."

To further illustrate quantitative and qualitative, below we share an example from our IA practice of examining a low-performing shopping cart in eCommerce. In this scenario, a team had quantitative data—the number of people who put an item in the cart and the number of completed purchases (called conversion rate). What they needed was qualitative data to add understanding to solve the problem, and the answer was surprising at the time.

eCommerce Shopping Cart Example

From the business point of view a shopping cart on eCommerce sites is where people place things for purchase. In this case, log analysis showed a lot of people were adding items and not completing a purchase—the numbers just didn't add up. Thus, a conclusion was drawn that the shopping cart was broken and a big redesign was needed. However, early research discovered the shopping cart was working just as expected... by the users! The design was functioning properly, but in fact the cart had many uses. Findings included:

- carts can be used as a place to save items for later review, and

- carts can be a place to calculate the final cost including shipping and taxes before deciding if the final total is acceptable.

Once these behaviors were discovered (neither of which involve completing a purchase), additional website features were designed. Today, in eCommerce we often see a "wish list" feature and shipping charges clearly displayed with products. Log analysis in this instance provided quantitative data around a problem, but not why it was occurring. Following up with qualitative research showed what was was happening, and suggested that expanded features were needed. The point is to not just discover what is happening; you must also try to understand why it occurs—the answers may surprise you.

4.1.3   USER PERSONAS

In addition to comprehensive research reports combining quantitative and qualitative data, personas can be a great way to share findings. User personas are fictional characters created to represent different user types that are based on the research. In other words, user personas are created via research, and consolidate and communicate the data into a representation of a user type. A persona has personal identifiers like a name, occupation, social status, interests, expectations, goals, stories, and tasks. The persona concept was first introduced to the user interface design field by Allan Cooper (2004) and can help IAs stay focused on the user, avoid designing for one's self, and avoid designing for needs that don't really exist.

Use of Personas

There are different practices in using personas.

- Using personas to create a rigorous form of user model, based on behavioral patterns that emerge from observational research. Personas can be used to represent the key behaviors, attitudes, skill levels, goals, work, and environment of real people. Personas also lay the foundation on which to build user flows and scenarios. The two are then used to guide the system's functionality and design.

- Conducting quantitative analysis based on personas to determine and prioritize system/product features to be built. Pruitt and Grudin (2003) use a "persona-weighted feature matrix" to help the development team to determine what features and capabilities the system should have.

- Using personas as a medium for communication. As described by Pruitt and Grudin (2003), while comprehensive user research reports provide valuable insights into design, many team members may not actually read them or end up remembering very little about them. When the results are represented by personas, team members are engaged more effectively. Personas utilize the power of narrative and storytelling to enhance attention, memory, and organization of detailed user data.

- Using personas is best when it is impossible to list exhaustively all the user types and characteristics. When there is a possibility to get complete statistics about users, a comprehensive user profiling approach might be more appropriate.

Benefits of Personas

A persona is both a design tool and a communication tool. Its main benefits include the following.

- Help team members share a specific, consistent understanding of various audience groups.

- Features or functions can be prioritized based on how well they address the needs of one or more personas.

- Provide a human "face" so as to focus empathy on the persons represented by the demographics.

- Create a good container to hold research data.

Personas Construction

Constructing personas is a dedicated process. Special attention is needed to:

- build personas around identified goals and behaviors based on the data. If rich data is not available, "proto-personas" based on assumptions may be considered, but do not confuse these with genuine personas;

- determine how much information can be fictional (like name or location) while still having the persona based on real data;

- avoid resume-like personas. Do not use separate personas with less data for communication with other teams, and a more comprehensive persona document for IAs and designers; and

- consider the persona and scenarios together, creating a "personario" by combining the two.

4.2   EVALUATION

Once we've designed a prototype or system, evaluation helps us see what we got right and what needs improvement. As critical as understanding the mission and objective before building a site or app can be, evaluation can investigate how well the design meets the business goals and user needs. Most importantly, it provides data to drive re-design efforts and continuous improvements.

4.2.1 THE NEED FOR EVALUATION

The paper "Evaluating Information Architecture," by Steve Toub (2000), although written many years ago, is still a good starting point, especially for understanding the challenges earlier design professionals faced when most organizations did not conduct evaluations. Toub clearly explains why evaluation is needed, its benefits, and the dangers of not assessing site information architecture (including lost revenue, lower productivity, and legal liability).

Compared to the situations described in the paper (no evaluation of IA), design practices have come a long way. More attention is being paid to the overall success of the user experience, organizations have adopted design guidelines, and digital design patterns have emerged. Many companies now have dedicated and well-trained information architects and designers. Successful companies such as Google and Amazon have entire teams gathering web usage data, analyzing user feedback, and tracking web metrics.

However, as we are all aware, there are still many poorly designed websites and apps that end up frustrating the user and causing business losses as well. Why is this the case? There are still many systems without clear visions and understanding about what their goals are and what their user needs are. Many systems still violate design guidelines and go against best practices. In addition, people's expectation of usability is getting higher and higher. When users have good experiences with well-designed websites or apps, they become less tolerant of poor design and they are more likely to reject those that are not up to date to today's usability standards.

4.3 RESEARCH AND EVALUATION METHODS

While it is important that IAs are familiar with all methods, and pick the ones that answer their research questions, some research and evaluation methods are used more frequently than others. Below we highlight several of those more commonly used.

4.3.1 HEURISTIC EVALUATION

Heuristic evaluation is a usability engineering technique that allows design professionals to identify design problems against a formal or informal set of design guidelines called heuristics. This technique has been widely used for website and other interactive system evaluations. The concept of heuristic evaluation was first developed by Jakob Nielsen based on his years of experience in usability before the web era (Nielsen and Mack, 1994). Nielsen has published several books and articles on website evaluation and is considered "the world's leading expert on web usability."

In a heuristic review, trained evaluators examine a system and note usability flaws, classifying them using the list of heuristics, and rating their severity from cosmetic to critical. After each evaluator rates the system individually, they meet and discuss their findings. Below we reproduce Nielsen's classic list of ten heuristics (available from: https://www.nngroup.com/articles/ten-usability-heuristics) that form the foundation of many IA heuristic evaluations.

Nielsen's 10 Usability Heuristics for User Interface Design (Nielsen, 1995)

1. Visibility of system status

2. Match between system and the real world

3. User control and freedom

4. Consistency and standards

5. Error prevention

6. Recognition rather than recall

7. Flexibility and efficiency of use

8. Aesthetic and minimalist design

9. Help users recognize, diagnose, and recover from errors

10. Help and documentation

4.3.2   USAGE STATISTICS AND LOG ANALYSIS

For most design projects, logs provide an abundance of information about how people use systems and where they run into problems. Even relatively simple tools can track visitor behaviors like pages visited and transactions. These data represent the real-world behavior and interests of the user. By analyzing the usage data, IAs can identify patterns of user behavior and intentions, assessing whether designs are fulfilling the intended purpose. The quantitative nature of the web usage data can empower IAs to communicate ideas and convince their business clients very effectively.

The following table comes from Diamond's article "Web Traffic Analytics and User Experience" (2003), which gives a list of possible metrics that are typically used for website analysis. Keep in mind, it is critical to select the metrics that are aligned with the site evaluation or redesign objectives.

Table 4.2: **Matrices for site evaluation** (from Diamond, 2003)		
Basic Site Metrics		
Overall Site Metrics	**Description**	**Reason**
Total site visits. Total site visitors/users.	Number of visits the site received. Number of individual visitors the site received (based on cookies).	Trending and basis of additional calculation.
Total site page views	Number of pages viewed on the site.	Trending and basis of additional calculation.
Average time spent per visit.	Usually a minutes: seconds of average visit length.	Trending and basis of comparison
Referring pages	Key sites/links that the user used to get to the site.	Strategic review of advertising, partnerships, and search engine optimization.
Page-level Metrics		
Visits/visitors to page	Number of visits and visitors each page received.	Trending and basis of additional calculation.
Page views	Number of page views each page received.	Trending and basis of additional calculation.
Visits to page as entry page	Number of visits to the page that were the first page view of the site.	Identify where users entered the site.
Visits to page as exit page	Number of visits to the page that were the last page view of the site.	Identify where and how users exit the site.
Average time spent on page	Length of time on average that was spent viewing this page.	Trending and basis of additional comparison.
Single access page [Bounce rate]	Number of visits to the site that included ONLY the page.	Identify whether page is useful, or is turning users away.
Clickstream	Pages looked at prior to and after target page.	Understand the links and user path to the core page.

Search logs can be used to get insights into design problems of the system. If logs show search is the most important feature of a site, that does not necessarily mean users are search dominant. Instead, a very likely reason could be that the users got so confused by the system's structure and navigation, and they used search as the last resort to find information. Navigation terms drawn from search logs are often used to improve labeling and navigation structures. With improved navigation, the users' reliance on search and help may go down dramatically.

Finally, it is important to be aware that, like any research method, log analysis has its own strengths and constraints. With the log data alone, you may get a good idea about what happened on the site but not necessarily why. You need to leverage multiple methods to achieve your goal. Interviews, usability studies, and other methods where you connect directly with users can help provide the reasons why.

4.3.3   CARD SORTING

Card sorting explores how users naturally group items together. Participants in these studies are given cards with terms on them that they put into categories. There are two types of card sorting. In an open card sort, users place the cards together in piles they create and name each pile as a new category. Categories are not predefined and users can create their own names for them. This is a good way to learn about how users naturally group content. In a closed sort, users place the cards into predefined categories. This is a good way to see if content fits well into the categories previously created. The two can be combined, conducting an open card sort to identify categories, then a closed card sort to see how well the categories work.

Card sorting is a relatively easy way to gather qualitative data about the organization of an information space. Using online tools, IAs can collect data and run analysis in an efficient manner with dozens of participants. Tree testing is the natural follow up to card sorting, and is used to evaluate the developed navigation structures.

4.3.4   USABILITY TESTING

Usability testing evaluates an information system by investigating its performance with real users. Testing may include prototypes (early, unfinished versions of the system—even paper prototypes) to help guide design and development, or the final product to see how well it works. During a usability test, IAs identify usability problems and collect data related to effectiveness, efficiency, and satisfaction (remember the ISO definition of usability from Chapter 3). Findings from the study can be compared to benchmarks or goals, and used to prioritize design strategies.

Generally speaking, in a usability test, IAs ask and answer the following questions.

- Are users are successful when completing tasks?

- What paths and workflows do people use to complete tasks?

- How long do tasks take to complete?

- How satisfied are users with the system?

• What are the recommendations for design changes and improvements?

Usability testing can be conducted in-person in a lab setting, remotely through online conferencing tools like Skype, or by using specialized research software. Sessions should be run often, each with a relatively modest number of participants depending on the research need (Nielsen, 2012). Usability tests are often combined with interviews, so the IA can learn more by asking about user behaviors observed during the session.

4.3.5   SURVEYS

Surveys are questionnaires sent to selected users in order to gather feedback from the questions they answer. Closed questions and open-ended questions are usually included. A closed question is one where the user has to choose from predefined answers, while an open-ended question allows the user to write their own response. Usually, open-ended gather qualitative data, answering "why" or "how" types of questions.

IAs should keep their surveys as short as possible while still collecting the required data. Doing so will increase the completion rate. Many survey tools are available online, providing options to reach wider audiences and making it more convenient for respondents. With any survey, validating questions before launching the study is necessary. Standardized questionnaires like the "System Usability Scale," or SUS (Brooke, 2013), are great tools to help create IA-effective surveys that produce quantitative results.

4.3.6   OBSERVATION AND CONTEXTUAL INQUIRY

In observation and contextual inquiry, IAs view users in a naturalistic setting, like their home or office, as they perform real work, not tasks created by the IA. Sometimes this is called "in the wild," because the IA leaves their workplace and travels to the user. Observation is excellent for getting a view of how users interact with integrated information spaces, without the constraints of a usability test.

Being observed is unnatural to many people and can influence behavior. To put the participant at ease it is sometimes recommended that sessions be structured in a master/apprentice format, where the IA takes on the role of apprentice learning how to do a job. Data collected in contextual inquiries often includes findings that would be impossible to collect with any other method, like observing printed instructions on a user's desk, seeing how they would contact a colleague for assistance, or noting how often they are interrupted in their workflow.

4.3.7   INTERVIEWS

During an interview, the researcher talks with an individual user face to face, over the phone, or via online channels. Before the session, IAs should write up a list of questions and follow-up probes, called a protocol. Sessions are usually recorded and transcribed, either in part or in full. User quotes are the data to be analyzed. Interviews are excellent for getting each participant's point of view, without influence from others as might happen in a group setting. This technique can stand on its own, or be combined with other methods, to capture qualitative data that supplement quantitative findings.

4.3.8   BENCHMARKING PROCESS

An important question to ask when you've completed a design is: How does it compare to other systems? We call this comparison "benchmarking." There are two main types of benchmarking. First, in competitive benchmarking you compare the system being designed to others in the same genre. Second, we can use before-and-after benchmarking. Here we compare different iterations of a system. After all the time and energy spent on a website redesign for example, what are the differences between the old and new? For example, will the new design be faster or more efficient for users, and what is the difference (maybe it is even slower)? Or, do people enjoy using it more? The benchmarking process can include many research methods like A/B testing, surveys, and usability testing, and more.

4.4   SUMMARY

Research and evaluation help IAs and their teams deliver systems that meet user needs and make sure that the systems perform as desired. There are many research methods available for the IA to use, and it is important to choose the right method(s) to answer questions about the user experience. Using research findings, IAs have the data needed to ensure users' goals and needs are met in design.

CHAPTER 5

Information Organization and Navigation Design

Information architects (IAs) spend a lot of time planning and designing organization and navigation systems. The ways people interact and navigate a website, app, or other information space greatly depends on content organization and relationships, and what kinds of navigation systems are implemented. In this chapter, we discuss organization and navigation systems together as they are closely related to each other.

To learn about organization and navigation systems, the first thing an IA should do is become familiar with the prevailing methods and techniques—many of which come from the library and information sciences. In general, to have good information architecture, one needs to consider the following components:

- **Logical Organization**

    e.g., alphabetic, numerical, and hierarchical organization schemas, as well as placement and labels

- **Semantic Organization**

    e.g., metadata, controlled vocabularies, content indexing, and tagging

- **Structural Navigation**

    e.g., global, local, and contextual navigation, process/wizard navigation, browsing aids, and site maps

- **Search**

    e.g., search algorithms, search result displays, search interfaces, and other search aids

Each of the components will be discussed below.

5.1 LOGICAL ORGANIZATION

One of our favorite references on organization systems is *The Order of Things: How Everything in the World is Organized ...into Hierarchies, Structures, and Pecking Order,* by Barbara A. Kipfer (1997). Kipfer provides ample examples of "naturally organized" structures for things "from the inner workings of the smallest things to the complex system of the universe." She shows that orders exist in nature and in our civilization. If we can identify the appropriate order and organize our knowledge accordingly, we can make every subject easier to understand and follow.

An important, yet often overlooked organization method is to identify and make use of the natural order: No matter the type of information spaces and subject area, there are certain order systems that appear natural and are easy for the user to follow. Here are some order systems used often.

- **Alphabetical**

  e.g., staff directory, department directory

- **Numerical**

  e.g., items sorted by price, distance, size, or other quantitative attributes

- **Chronological**

  e.g., time-sensitive resources such as news articles sorted by date

- **Geographical**

  e.g., information that can be easily attached to geographical locations

- **By tasks**

  e.g., user goals or needs

- **By audience types**

  e.g., a university website is organized by audience types: faculty, current students, prospective students, and alumni

- **By metaphor**

  e.g., rainbows of colors, solar systems, and other things that have apparent natural order

- **By popularity or usage frequency**

  e.g., instead of being based on pre-determined order, the sequence changes dynamically based on usage or participation, such as most popular, highest rated, or frequently visited

- **By relevance**

e.g., depends on the way the relevance is calculated, it can be based on a combination of several of the above methods

- **Personalization and customization**

e.g., based on personal preferences or user settings

All these methods have an "order" that can be defined systematically. For information organization, IAs need to decide which of these methods to implement and let users understand how it was used to organize the content and the display, so they may easily find what they want. Figure 5.1 shows an ordered list of university undergraduate majors, illustrating how logical order can help users find things (like locating the "history" major).

▶ Anthropology	College of Arts and Sciences
▶ Biological Sciences	College of Arts and Sciences
▶ Chemistry	College of Arts and Sciences
▶ Communication	College of Arts and Sciences
▶ Criminology and Justice Studies	College of Arts and Sciences
▶ Emerging Scholars Program	College of Arts and Sciences
▶ English	College of Arts and Sciences
▶ Environmental Science	College of Arts and Sciences
▶ Environmental Studies and Sustainability	College of Arts and Sciences
▶ Geoscience	College of Arts and Sciences
▶ Global Studies	College of Arts and Sciences
▶ History	College of Arts and Sciences
▶ Mathematics	College of Arts and Sciences
▶ Philosophy	College of Arts and Sciences
▶ Physics	College of Arts and Sciences
▶ Political Science	College of Arts and Sciences
▶ Psychology	College of Arts and Sciences
▶ Sociology	College of Arts and Sciences
▶ Undeclared – General Humanities and Social Sciences	College of Arts and Sciences
▶ Undeclared – Science	College of Arts and Sciences

Figure 5.1: A listing of the undergraduate majors in Drexel University's College of Arts and Sciences. Notice how the organization is alphabetical, making the list easily scannable.

5.2   SEMANTIC ORGANIZATION

The above list could also include a method called "by content," but content is hardly a simple "order" that can be defined clearly, so we separate it from others. Organizing by content is to organize by *semantic relationships* of the content—that is, to organize it by its meaning.

Semantic organization is one of the most important organization methods for information architecture, and has its own descriptive languages and methods. Following, we discuss four major methods of semantic organization: metadata, controlled vocabulary, faceted classification, and social classification.

5.2.1   METADATA

Metadata is "structured information that describes, explains, locates, or otherwise makes it easier to retrieve, use, or manage an information resource" (NISO, 2004). Developing metadata is often the first step to getting information organized.

Metadata, sometimes called "the data about data," treats data as a describable "digital object" and describes the object in term of its content, context, and structure (Gilliland-Swetland et al., 2000).

- "Content relates to what the object contains or is about."

- "Context indicates the who, what, why, where, how aspects associated with the object's creation."

- "Structure relates to the formal set of associations within or among individual information objects."

Another way of thinking about metadata could be "the data about the content," "the data about the information," or "the data about the resource." The key to helping understand this topic, we've found as teachers, is for our students to not overthink when starting out. It is very easy to get caught up with advanced theories and concepts when first learning about metadata. In fact, metadata can be something as simple as "title=bookTitle." However, to make metadata useful we need to take a structured approach, starting with looking at the kinds of metadata IAs use. NISO (2004) describes the three main types of metadata:

1. **Descriptive metadata** describes an information resource

   e.g., title=Drexel University

2. **Structural metadata** describes the types, versions, and relationships of information object

   e.g., section=1, chapter=5, page=3

3. **Administrative metadata** gives technical and other information to help manage the information resource

   e.g., source=documentScanner123

Along with its different types, metadata has many important characteristics. These characteristics help make metadata useful and easy to create, maintain, and understand. For IA, two should be emphasized in particular: standardization and indexing quality.

Standardization

Standardization means the creators and users of metadata agree to use a shared set of elements. A common metadata standard, Dublin Core Metadata Set (DC) defines 15 metadata elements (Table 5.1) that can be used to describe many types of information resources. As simple as they may look, these elements provide a much-needed structure. Everyone who uses DC agrees to abide by the rules of the standard, which lets other people and computers understand, use, and share metadata, making information resources easier to manage and extend.

Table 5.1: Dublin Core elements, v 1.1. http://www.dublincore.org/documents/dces/	
DC Elements	**Definitions**
Contributor	An entity responsible for making contributions to the resource.
Coverage	The spatial or temporal topic of the resource, the spatial applicability of the resource, or the jurisdiction under which the resource is relevant.
Creator	An entity primarily responsible for making the resource.
Date	A point or period of time associated with an event in the lifecycle of the resource.
Description	An account of the resource.
Format	The file format, physical medium, or dimensions of the resource.
Identifier	An unambiguous reference to the resource within a given context.
Language	A language of the resource.
Publisher	An entity responsible for making the resource available.
Relation	A related resource.
Rights	Information about rights held in and over the resource.
Source	A related resource from which the described resource is derived.
Subject	The topic of the resource.
Title	A name given to the resource.
Type	The nature or genre of the resource.

Standardization supports an important feature of metadata, that it is readable by humans and also "readable" by computer. Using the DC standard (or other standards), an IA provides metadata that can be processed by computers because the data is in a format computer programs are developed to interpret. For example, with the "language" element, an IA can assign Spanish, so that a computer system can deliver only web pages that have "lang=Spanish" in their metadata for a request from Spain; and for a human user the interface displays controls to the effect of, "show me this page in Spanish."

The Dublin Core metadata standard was based on traditional library's cataloging principles. Much of the information technology industry learned about it soon after its creation, leading to its popular use. DC metadata elements are now often parts of many other metadata standards—it was published as ISO standard 15836 in 2009. Many other leading information organizations also maintain metadata standards for their specific topic areas. The Library of Congress produces several important library metadata standards, including PREMIS, METS, and MODS available at https://www.loc.gov/standards/.

Indexing Quality

The second function of metadata is to improve the quality of indexing, which is often a main motivation for using metadata in systems with a search function or that will be searchable online. On the web, since search engines factor metadata terms into their results, rankings, and displays, adding appropriate metadata terms can improve a web page's retrievability and findability. Recall that NISO's metadata definition includes making the resource easier to find and retrieve. It is interesting to note that the original motivation of having DC metadata was to promote metadata standards, its usefulness in improving indexing quality helps make it more practical and widely accepted.

A bottleneck of metadata application is still the difficulty in generating it automatically. While a lot of progress has been made for automatic metadata creation, most is still created through a manual process. Content management systems help generate and manage metadata as part of the content creation process, lessening the effort in some cases. Investigation into automatic metadata generation from content is an ongoing research area.

5.2.2   CONTROLLED VOCABULARIES

Other than standard elements, metadata systems have no specific content structures. For specific domains, additional content structures can be added through controlled vocabularies or thesauri, which describe the terms to be used as descriptors in a knowledge domain. A descriptor is a unique term assigned to one, and only one, concept in the domain.

Controlled vocabularies are a collection of terms selected and organized by domain experts to represent concepts in a specific domain of knowledge following general guidelines. Every concept covered within the domain will be assigned a unique term (called descriptor, subject term, or preferred term). Other terms with similar meanings will be called equivalent terms, lead-in terms, or synonyms. The relationships between descriptors are established through hierarchical relationships such as Broader Term (BT) and Narrower Term (NT), and associative relationships such as Related Term (RT). Let's take a look at an example from eCommerce:

Descriptor: Shirts

- Broader Term (BT): Clothing

- Narrower Terms (NT): T-Shirts, Dress Shirts, Polo Shirts

- Related Terms (RT): Tops, Blouses

Using the example above, an eCommerce search engine could find or suggest items for a user's search, even if the keywords do not exactly match the descriptor. A search for "tops" could return "shirts," whereas if tops was not related to shirts through the RT relationship, then the search would fail. If you've ever searched or browsed an eCommerce site, you've interacted with a controlled vocabulary.

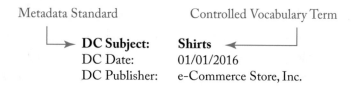

Figure 5.2: Element from a metadata standard (left), and the value from a controlled vocabulary (right). Only values that are in the controlled vocabulary can be assigned to an element.

Controlled vocabularies establish a precise mapping between a term/label and a concept, reducing ambiguity caused by homographs, synonyms, polysemes, and other problems existing in natural languages. Once controlled vocabularies are created, entries in them can be used as subject terms in metadata to index resources.

Advantages of Controlled Vocabularies

There are several advantages of using controlled vocabularies with metadata. First, the content will be represented more precisely through the carefully selected terms. Second, term relationships established in the controlled vocabularies will add an additional content-based navigation structure like hierarchies, which are very helpful for users' browsing activities. Third, indexing and searching precision will be greatly improved through the terms and relationship structures inherent in controlled vocabularies.

Disadvantages of Controlled Vocabularies

Disadvantages of controlled vocabularies include the labor-intensive creation process, and the difficulty to maintain and update the vocabularies. In the online environment in particular, controlled vocabularies are sometimes replaced by *taxonomies*. Taxonomies are generally organized hierarchically or poly-hierarchically. The hierarchy can be mixed—not necessary strictly broader/narrower relationships; cross-references can be defined and terms can be added or deleted more easily than in a true controlled vocabulary.

Faceted Classification

A special, more structured type of taxonomy is Faceted Classification, used by many IAs who are organizing websites or search tools (Tunkelang, 2009). We see these quite often in online ecommerce and library systems. By definition, faceted classification classifies information objects by concepts from multiple orthogonal categories (called facets). Orthogonal means "mutually exclusive," and is fundamental to faceted classification. This means facets cannot overlap. Ideally, each facet should also be a complete description of the area it covers. An information object can be described by one and only one category within each facet (for example, a particular item in eCommerce cannot be both a shirt and pants). But in practice, both orthogonality and completeness might be difficult to achieve. Many eCommerce sites, libraries, and other organizations adopted faceted classification to provide additional "access points" to their holdings, meaning labels or terms that can be used to find objects.

The following example (Figure 5.3), from the Philadelphia Free Library, gives a good example of faceted classification. Here we can see on the left several facets used as filters that help guide a user to the item they want (e.g., show only eBooks). Notice that facets expose some of the system's descriptive, structural, and administrative metadata.

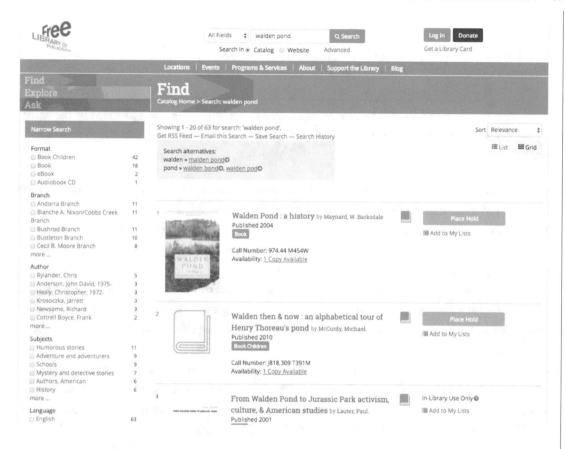

Figure 5.3: Faceted classification used in a public library system.

Tagging and Social Classification

Over the past decade, users' ability to organize digital information according to their own notions has attracted a lot of attention in the information architecture and related communities. Particularly in social media, tagging (Trant, 2009) and social classification, or social curation (Zarro and Hall, 2012), has become an integral part of the user experience in many information systems. Although organizing information in a way geared toward user needs is not necessarily new, providing users the tools to easily and publicly classify information objects with their own labels is a new capability supported by digital technologies. Contrasted to professionally developed, well-structured, hierarchical taxonomies and controlled vocabularies, social classification results in unstructured categories that are free of "control." Users can select and decide to use whatever terms they like to tag web pages, images, social media posts, and so on. Uniformity and organizing power emerge from the collective categorizing activities of the user community.

Figure 5.4: Tags or hashtags added to a user's post on Twitter. Notice the terms preceded by the hash symbol (#) are hyperlinks. Clicking them will open a results page with other tweets that have been similarly tagged.

Unsurprisingly, there have been different schools of thought on tagging. Previously, some IAs thought that user-generated tagging structures (called "folksonomies," a term coined by Thomas Vander Wal) could replace taxonomies. However, tagging appears to be more useful as a complement to taxonomies. Tags offer new ways for people to find, discover, and share information resources—particularly in emergent or popular culture topics where terms may not be a part of previously developed vocabularies or taxonomies. Organizations like the Library of Congress and Smithsonian have even used tagging and social media posts to identify digital photos in their collections and to provide terms that were added to their catalog (Kalfatovic et al., 2009; Springer et al., 2008).

The downside of tagging is messiness, tagging motivation issues, scalability, and global applicability (Guy and Tonkin, 2006). Tags created by a user may be very personal (e.g. "read_later"), misspelled, or not applicable to a wide audience (Marlow et al., 2006). Even with these limitations, tagging has become an important part of today's digital landscape.

In the following, we highlight several advantages of tagging and social classification in the context of information architecture.

Tagging is More Flexible, with Lower Cognitive Cost than Categorization

Tagging allows the user to describe an object in their own terms, while professional cataloging usually requires fitting the object to one unique location in a hierarchy (sometimes it is necessary, e.g., each book in the library needs to have a unique physical location). Multiple tags provide additional access points, which may match other users' concepts of an object. Also, tagging is easier and more enjoyable than categorization because tagging is a two-step process while classification involves three steps (Sinha, 2005).

Simple tagging is available in the form of "hashtags" which are terms preceded by the hash (or pound) symbol (Figure 5.4). Hashtags are used in many social networking tools as a way to quickly label content or images. Some Twitter hashtags related to IA topics of interest include: *#ia #informationarchitecture #ux #userexperience #hci #designthinking*. The "#ia" tag demonstrates the messiness in tagging. A search for #ia on Twitter shows the hashtag is used by different groups for unrelated purposes. #ia is a homonym—used for both information architecture and tweets related to the state of Iowa (commonly abbreviated as IA). Ambiguity in tagging means that the system does not know the intent of the user, it simply applies the label. The curious IA, or Iowan, is left to filter through tweets of both related and unrelated interests.

Another way to explain the low cognitive cost of tagging is through its easy-to-use interfaces. Figure 5.5 shows a Twitter tagging interface. Several features of this interface are popular among tagging interfaces. For example, (1) the interface automatically fills in the known data when the user opens up this tagging interface (in this case, by entering the hash symbol); (2) it shows a list of recommended tags, and users can click on any of tags in the lists to tag add the tag; (3) it provides the type-ahead function. All these features contribute to an easy-to-use interface, making the tagging process almost effortless. Other interfaces are shown in Figure 5.6, a tagging in Pinterest.com, while Figure 5.7 shows the tagging interface from the web2.0 site delicious.com.

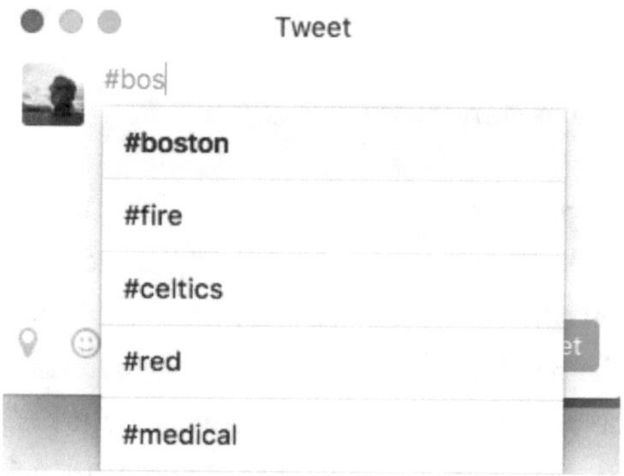

Figure 5.5: Adding tags in the Twitter interface.

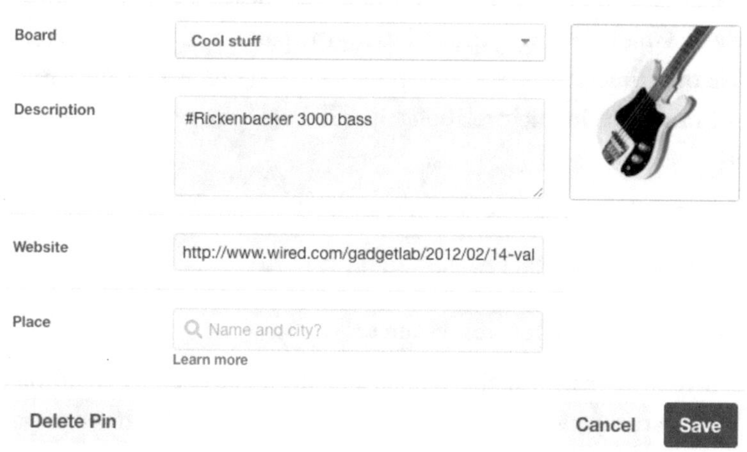

Figure 5.6: Tagging in the Pinterest interface.

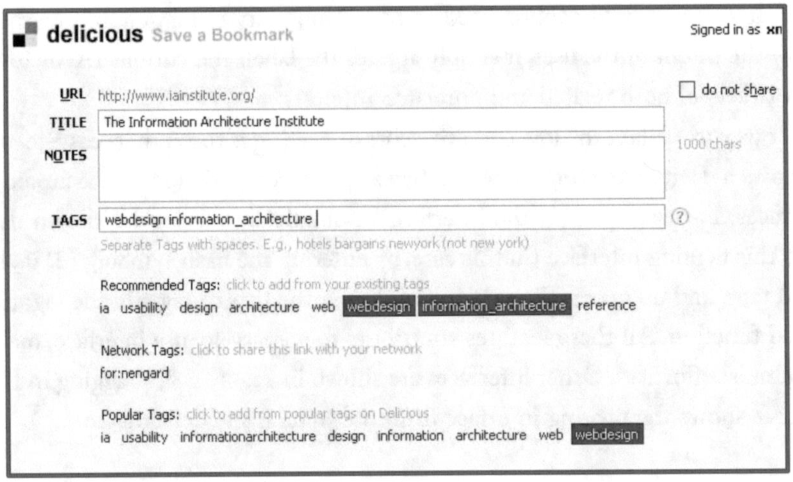

Figure 5.7: Tagging in the delicious.com interface.

In addition, in many tagging systems, each user's resulting tags and tagging frequencies automatically make up personal collections, which over time dynamically reveal the structure of the user's interests and their personal collections (objects they have tagged). Personal collections also serve as an emergent navigation schema—instead of following a predetermined hierarchy to navigate, the user can navigate through the system via a dynamic network built through shared interests. Person A can see Person B's tags, and vice-versa, allowing them to navigate using each other's tags or labels.

Collective Intelligence

Although a major motivation of tagging in a social classification system is for personal use, according to a study by Golder and Huberman (2006) the pattern of tag usage emerges rather early and remains stable over time. A valuable side-product of tagging is that the aggregation statistics also reveal a lot of otherwise implicit relationships. The user can often see immediate system aggregation results.

- How many people have tagged this resource?

- What tags have been applied to this resource?

- Who has used what tags for this resource?

Aggregation tells the user whether this is a popular resource (it could be an indicator of quality or value), what are the most popular tags for this resource, and who shares the same interest as me. From here a user could use the tags to navigate to other resources that have been similarly tagged, or in some systems view a public profile of others, to see what else they have tagged.

Users can also utilize one known resource as navigation to other relevant resources via shared tags, similar to citation-based information retrieval (backward and forward citation chaining) in the library sciences. CiteULike.com applied this mechanism for academic resource sharing and organization as an efficient way to discover new resources. Shared tags also contribute to a positive user experience—it allows the user to benefit from others' tagging via his or her participation.

In summary, tagging represents a user-centered approach to information organization. Rather than building "trees" as in traditional classification systems and taxonomies, tagging creates "piles of leaves," relying on the power of networks, search engines, and collective intelligence to get the order out of the piles. User-created labels complement the traditional classification performed by experts as shown in Figure 5.8. By using them together, IAs can sometimes get the best of both worlds.

> **Categories and Subject Descriptors**
> H.3.5 [Information Storage and Retrieval]: On-line information services – Web-based services
>
> **General Terms**
> Design, Human Factors, Standardization.
>
> **Keywords**
> Social collecting, annotations, linking, sharing, Pinterest.

Figure 5.8: Taxonomic category terms, general vocabulary terms, and user chosen tags/keywords for an article in the ACM digital library. The paper described here explores user activities on the social media site Pinterest.com, which is reflected only in the user-supplied tags/keywords.

5.3   NAVIGATION SYSTEMS

5.3.1   PURPOSE OF NAVIGATION

The purpose of navigation is to help users move around, reach the information they want, and show their context or location. Using the physical building metaphor, we can say structuring and organizing information is about creating rooms and producing floor plans whereas navigation is about adding ways to move about: doors, stairs, elevators, and hallways. Navigation adds meaningful connections to the organization structures, facilitating task completion. Because the user comes to a system with different motivations, IAs often need to provide multiple ways for navigation.

To create good navigation, help the user answer the following questions.

1. Where am I? (orientation)

2. What can I do? (content, interaction, search)

3. Where can I go from here?

    a. Drill up

    b. Parallel move at the same level

    c. Drill down

Navigation Types

Navigation can be within one information space, across several information spaces, or the entire digital landscape. Web browsers, mobile apps, search engines, aggregators and directories, and social media provide different types of navigation for people to navigate the whole web domain. For information architects, navigation design often focuses on within-site/app navigation, such as:

- global navigation and sectional navigation;

- local navigation;

- supplemental navigation; or

- process navigation.

Figure 5.9 illustrates typical locations of major navigation types in a desktop website.

Global and Sectional Navigation

Global navigation brings together the key set of access points that users might need to get from one end of the site to the other. Anywhere you want to go, you can get there (eventually) from the global navigation (when users get lost, they often go back to the global navigation and start over again).

Local Navigation

Local navigation includes page-level navigation and contextual navigation. *Page-level navigation* helps the user easily move around different sections of the page. On descriptive pages there could be an overview/anchor links on the top or on the side, back to top links, etc. For pages with large data-sets (e.g., a search results page) UI elements should be available for comparing, sorting, and selecting.

    Contextual navigation follows content and context, rather than structures. The links are usually embedded in the context of the content (via inline links) or displayed in a specific area of the page (e.g., associative links for related items), commonly seen on the right-hand side, on the upper right corner, or at the bottom of the page. This type of navigation supports associative learning.

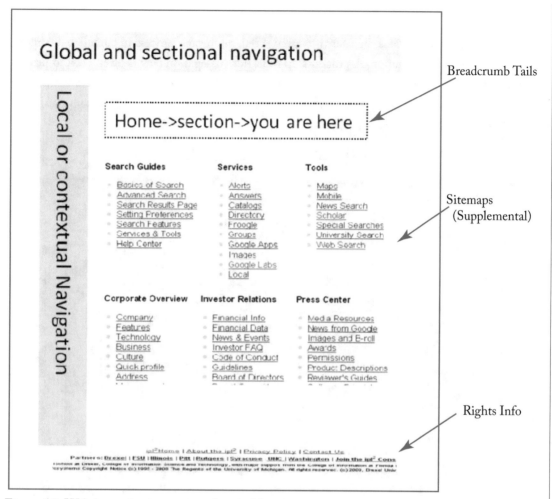

Figure 5.9: Website navigation types and typical locations.

Supplemental Navigation

Typical examples of supplemental navigation include sitemaps, site indexes, breadcrumb trails, FAQs, special guides, or tutorials. Sitemaps and site indexes were more commonly seen in early websites. Sitemaps are generally considered a top-down approach to content organization while site indexing is a bottom-up approach. Thus, sitemaps emphasize overview functions where site indexing will provide more details (Fox, 2003). Paul Kahn collected many examples of sitemaps, and he divided them into different categories such as manually created vs. data-driven, text-only vs. graphical, and 2-D vs. 3-D (Kahn and Lenk, 2001).

Process Navigation

Finally, navigation that guides the user through a serial, multi-step process to complete a complex task is called process navigation. A process step indicator (navigation bar) is often used to provide an overview to users about where they are and what they need to go through to finish the process.

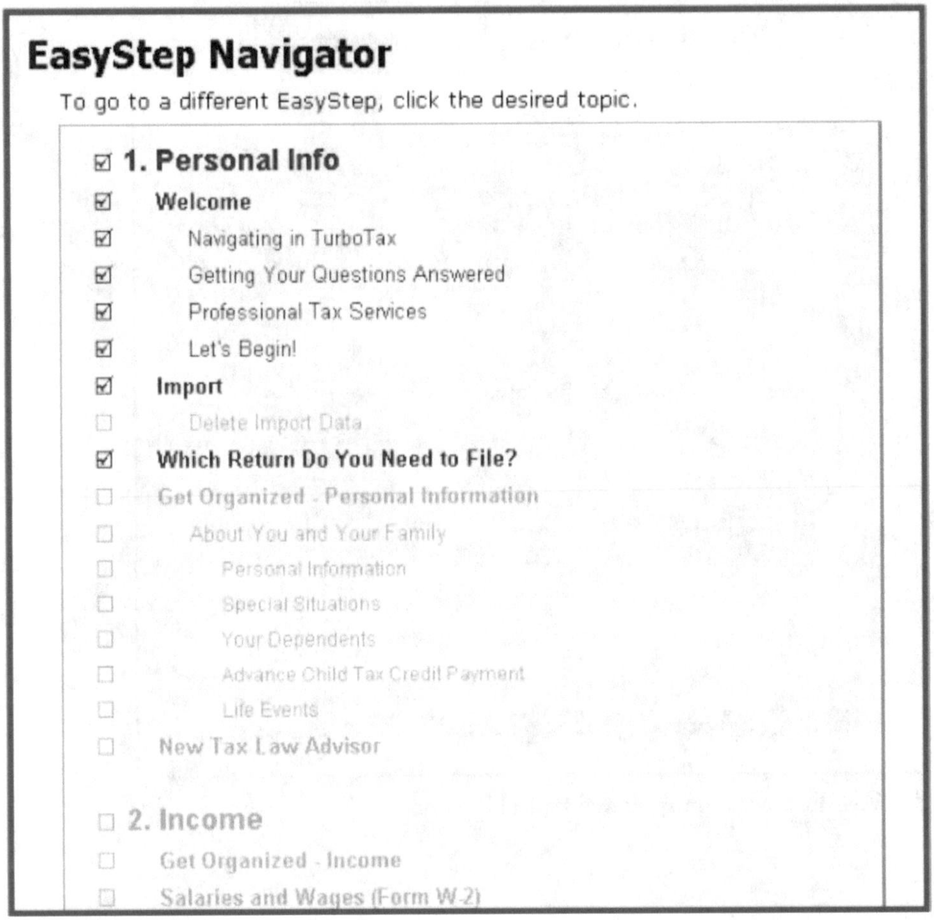

Figure 5.10: Turbo Tax process navigation.

Figure 5.10 shows an older version of TurboTax's navigation for helping a user complete their tax returns. As you can see, it follows steps from basic personal information, to more detailed income. Simpler process navigation may only contain "Cancel" (or "Back") and "Continue" (or "Next") buttons. This type of navigation is task-flow oriented, helping the user concentrate on the particular flow, in this case completing a tax return. If process navigation is used in transactional flows, like an eCommerce checkout, the global navigation of the site could appear at the beginning and the end of the process but is often hidden during the process.

5.4   SEARCH SYSTEMS

Searching is a means for the user to access information, web pages, or files using keyword queries. With a search engine, users can bring related pages (pages that match the search query) together instantly by entering keywords and then browsing through the results. However, having a good search engine alone does not guarantee that the user will be successful.

There are many factors that will significantly impact the user's searching behavior.

- First, users need to know what they need. This turns out to be the most difficult problem for information retrieval. A lot of times, users just have a problem to solve. They do not know what information will help them solve the problem. In other words, they do not know what they are searching for.

- Second, users need to express their needs in queries. Queries stated in a few words (most queries are one to three terms) are not the best way to represent one's information needs (Belkin et al., 1982). Still, that has been the way people have used search engines for many years.

- Third, the search engine needs to index content appropriately, but there is no one optimized indexing method that will work best for all users' queries.

- Fourth, the search results need to be displayed in a way that users understand. For an in-depth discussion on the display, Hearst's book *Search User Interfaces* (2009), also available online as a free e-Book, is a good introduction.

There are a lot of misunderstandings about the role of search engines. As an information architect, one big challenge is to communicate to content owners and users what search engines can and cannot do. Here is just a short summary of some potential misunderstanding of search engines.

- *It is not there if I cannot find it through search engines.* Many users might think this way. They assume that each site has an optimal search engine for their information needs. In fact a search may fail for many reasons, including problems in queries, query mapping process, indexing scope, and vocabulary matching.

- *Users can always use search engines to find what they want.* This is an excuse for not doing a good navigation design. Research indicates that user's success rate with search engines can be quite poor (even less than 50%).

- *All we need is to have Google on our site.* Google is currently the dominant search engine. But its real advantage lies in its indexing of the web as a whole; it may not work as well as it should on a single site. For example, Google's algorithm relies partially on a "popularity contest" for query matching and query result ranking. A site may not appropriate "popularity" data.

In short, search cannot solve wayfinding problems in websites, apps, enterprise software—or any information space. Search and navigation should work together to support information retrieval needs. Peter Morville's books *Ambient Findability* (2005) and *Search Patterns* (Morville and Callender, 2010) are excellent places to explore more about IA and search.

5.5   SUMMARY

Organizing information spaces is a fundamental part of information architecture. Luckily, IAs can draw from the library sciences and other areas for understanding and best practices, like using logical organization structures. Controlled vocabularies, taxonomies, and faceted search are used by IAs to provide top-down structure, while tagging and social classification give users powerful ways to add bottom-up organization—matching a wide range of user concepts to information resources. This can prove particularly useful in emerging areas where professional categorization may not exist. Navigation and search help users traverse through spaces to find information. The tradeoffs inherent in navigation, and search design and technologies, mean the IA should strive to understand user needs and develop optimal strategies matching those needs, while accepting that no strategy will ever be perfect.

CHAPTER 6

User Information Behavior and Design Implications

Human information behavior (HIB) is, like organization systems, its own field of study with a rich history. The study of HIB includes an individual's or group's actions and interactions with any information source: other people, books and libraries, mass media, and many others. Just the fact we are sentient beings receiving stimuli from our environment means information behavior is a constant presence in our lives—we are constantly processing and using information (you're doing it right now!).

> **Information Behavior** *is the totality of human behavior in relation to sources and channels of information, including both active and passive information seeking, and information use. Thus, it includes face-to-face communication with others, as well as the passive reception of information as in, for example, watching TV advertisements, without any intention to act on the information given* (Wilson, 2000).

Information behavior is independent of information technology, even though behaviors are shaped by the technologies available. While the underlying psychology and biology of information behavior in a human being may remain the same, the *observable behaviors* will change in response to emerging and evolving channels or technology. For example, today we would not study someone's interaction with a network of friends and family by getting a list of all the people they've mailed physical letters—rather we would investigate their email, chat, and social media.

HIB is more than thinking about designing wireframe screens or user flows for a single application. Considering a wide range of HIB during the creation and design of an information system will provide guidance for design decisions and help develop questions for user research. In earlier chapters, we emphasized that there is nothing more important than user research in the IA and UCD process. We also examined various methods for user research and usability evaluation as well as their uses in different scenarios. In this chapter, we discuss how to apply certain empirical findings resulting from foundational research to IA design. There are two types of empirical data IAs can use.

1. **Primary Research:** The findings and recommendations based on your own research in a very specific context (for your project).

2. **Secondary Research:** Research findings and guidelines that are widely acknowledged or adopted in the industry, or reported in academic papers.

While the former takes precedence in a specific design project our focus here is on the latter, which can be generalized across all of IA. Note, these findings and guidelines either come from repeated empirical studies and/or are based on theories and principles from information science, HCI, and other related disciplines. Experienced IAs take advantage of both primary and secondary research to inform and drive their designs.

6.1   UNDERSTANDING USER NEEDS AND INFORMATION BEHAVIOR

Why do we need to spend so much time and energy trying to understand users? For two main reasons.

1. You are not your users. Be extremely cautious when making assumptions about users. By learning about them through research, IAs make more data-driven decisions.

2. Users are diverse—their demographics, goals, attitudes, behaviors, preferences, knowledge, skills, social contexts, and many other characteristics can be distinctive, all of which influence design. This is where user personas can come into play: identify and prioritize user types. Create scenarios and flows for each user type, and try to learn as much as possible about your users in context.

Users are also the same—sharing many traits defined by human emotion, psychology, and cognition. In this chapter we look at some of the information behaviors intrinsic to humans.

6.2   THEORIES AND PRINCIPLES ABOUT USER INFORMATION BEHAVIOR

In this section, we will introduce several theories and principles that have become influential in the IA, HCI, and UX domains. You may notice similarities between some theories, and how others may be combined to help form a broader picture of human users. Some are concerned with what is happening within the mind of the user, and their limitations, while others look more at behavioral aspects.

6.2.1   MAGIC NUMBER SEVEN

Miller's (1956) "magic number seven, plus or minus two" demonstrates some of the limitations humans have in terms of memory. (Miller's article was republished on the web and at press is available here http://cogprints.org/730/1/miller.html.)

The central argument for our purposes is that the average human can only hold seven, plus or minus two, chunks of information in short-term memory. The point here is not to always limit choices to seven items, but rather to consider this law when expecting people to recall information, and to know that humans have limits. This helps explain why phone numbers were broken up into the pattern 555-555-5555, as this could be seen as three chunks, not 10. By presenting a phone number as three chunks, it is more easily recalled later.

However, we do not want to blindly follow this concept in IA. How does 7 +/- 2 relate to something like menus on a website? Human beings can only remember a limited amount of information; we are much better at recognition. Might that be why something like large dropdown menus (mega menus), which may seem like they violate 7 +/-2, are effective? Users recognize the labels used, they do not recall them from memory.

6.2.2   HICK'S LAW

Hick's Law, also called the Hick-Hyman Law (Hick, 1952; Hyman, 1953), describes the amount of time it takes for a human to make a decision, as a function of all of the choices present: the time it takes to make a decision increases as more alternatives are available. Hick's law is mainly useful for simple decision making; as complexity increases the applicability of the law decreases (Lidwell et al., 2003). The law can be useful when designing for simple, time-sensitive decisions; limit the number of choices.

6.2.3   ZIPF'S LAW: THE PRINCIPLE OF LEAST EFFORT

Zipf's Law is also thought of as the principle of least effort in IA. In Zipf's words (1949), "Every individual when considering a course of action, will choose the action that requires the least amount of effort." This principle has been widely cited in the library and information science literature to explain user information-seeking behaviors. There are two well-known conclusions based on this principle. One is the 80/20 rule: among all the information sources available, people use 20% of them for 80% of their information needs. The other conclusion is people will choose easily available information sources of relatively low quality over expending the effort necessary to access higher quality sources.

Rather than complaining that people are lazy, we should acknowledge that users are efficiency-driven. From a design perspective, it could also help us prioritize user tasks and goals. At the same time, we need to understand this is a strategy for survival but not for excellence. It may not apply to all situations.

6.2.4   INFORMATION SCENT THEORY

Information Foraging/Scent Theory, proposed at Xerox PARC (Pirolli and Card 1999; Card et al., 2001), has been widely adopted for design (and it is quite similar to the berry-picking model). Pirolli and Card (1999) uses the analogy of wild animals gathering food to analyze how humans collect information. Like wild animals making optimal decisions on where, when, and how to eat, "informavores" (information seekers) constantly make decisions on what kind of information to look for: whether to stay at the current location, when to move to on, which link to follow, and when to finally stop. The decision is made such that the user gets maximum benefit for minimum effort (like the least effort principle).

One of the important concepts of information foraging is "information scent." Information scent is used to predict a path's success. In other words, it is used to describe how people evaluate options when they are looking for information on a website. When presented with a list of options users will choose the one that gives them the clearest indication (or strongest scent) that it will take them closer to the information they require. "Informavores" will keep clicking as long as they sense that they are "getting warmer"—the scent must keep getting stronger and stronger or they will give up.

6.2.5   BOUNDED RATIONALITY

Herb Simon, an economics researcher and Nobel laureate, coined the term "bounded rationality" (1996). Bounded rationality is about the constraints people face, both external and internal, when making a decision. The perfect choice is rarely made—usually there is some compromise—people must "satisfice." With unlimited time and unlimited resources, everyone could make better decisions—but that is not reality, there are always limitations. So a person makes a decision that is "rational" within the "boundaries" of their situation. Examples of limits/bounds in IA include:

- the information people have available to them,

- cognitive abilities, and

- limited time to make a decision.

Part of the IA's job is to recognize the ability and limitations of the users in context. Often concepts like bounded rationality point the way toward questions to ask in user research, and toward requirements in design.

6.2.6   DUAL PROCESS THEORY

Dual process theory, which was developed from research on trust and persuasion in the social psychology domain, provides further insights into the motivations and actions of a user (Chaiken, 1980; Petty and Cacioppo, 1986). Humans store rules, called heuristics (but not the same as Nielsen's 10 heuristics), in their memory that are then used to evaluate information and information sources in whole or in part. An example heuristic for IA is "the first result in a search results page is the best." Humans also engage in "systematic processing," which is careful reading and analysis of an information resource, bounded by limitations like time or motivation. Information processing exists on a continuum between heuristics and systematic processing.

6.2.7   PARADOX OF CHOICE: LESS IS MORE

The book *Paradox of Choice: Why Less Is More,* by Barry Schwartz (2004), has been widely referenced by the design community. Schwartz identifies two types of people based on their decision-making patterns.

- **Maximizers:** Trying to make the best possible decision.

- **Satisficers:** Selecting the first one meeting minimal requirements. (Note that Simon also used the term satisficing in his exploration of bounded rationality.)

While satisficers are content to select products or services that meet a minimum set of requirements, maximizers compare all possible options. According to Schwartz, when there is no choice life is miserable; but with too many choices, other issues come up.

- **Analysis Paralysis:** When there are so many choices, you end up not being able to make a choice quickly. A grocery store did an experiment with two treatments. One was to allow customers to sample 24 or 6 different flavors of jam. With 24 options, more people came to the table but 1/10th as many people actually bought jam than the other setting.

- **Decision Quality:** With too many choices, the decision-making process gets exponentially more complex. People tend to adopt the most simple and avoid the complex criteria, but simple ones aren't necessarily the most important criteria. As a result, they end up making a worse decision.

- **Decision Satisfaction:** Doing better and feeling worse. If you managed to overcome paralysis and ensure decision quality, satisfaction is the third factor. When there are more choices, it becomes easier to regret—satisfaction is reduced. If you did not examine ALL options, you assume one or more other options might have been better.

- **Opportunity Cost:** Even though you made the right decision, there is no easy way to tell this is truly better than your next best alternative. That will make you feel less satisfied with your choice: "Everything suffers from comparison."

- **Escalation of Expectations:** Seeing more choices raises expectations. When your expectation is higher than the selection, you experience regret. Schwartz gave an example: In a study on college seniors looking for jobs, maximizers got jobs with $7,500 more or 25% higher for their salary, but they felt worse (and were also more pessimistic, overwhelmed, stressed, and disappointed) than the satisficers.

How to Cope with Too Many Choices?

From the designer's perspective, here are the things you can do to help the user.

- Create default settings aligned with users' best interests, because people tend to do nothing when facing multiple choices.

- Use invisible filters (e.g., based on previous behavior, profile preferences) and visible filters (allowing the user to articulate their selection criteria) to limit choices for the user.

- Organize choices hierarchically—because hierarchical structure feels smaller than flat lists so the number of choices is perceived as fewer.

6.2.8   THE BERRY PICKING INFORMATION BEHAVIOR MODEL

Marcia Bates' berry-picking model (1989) is well known in the library and information science field. It has been used to explain the pattern of exploratory information discovery and was introduced to IA by Rosenfeld and Morville. According to Bates, interesting information is scattered like berries in the bushes. A search query, therefore is continually shifting; users may move through a variety of sources; new information may yield new ideas and new directions; the query is not satisfied by a single last retrieved set of results, but rather by a series of selections and bits of information found along the way. A searcher in this model is "moving through many actions toward a general goal of satisfactory completion of research related to an information need."

6.2.9   EXPLORATORY SEARCH

Exploratory search (Marchionini, 2006) shows how searching can take place over an extended period of time. The searcher learns as they go, and this learning influences subsequent search sessions. It is sometimes described as searching and browsing combined, because we are looking at search not as a tool but as the satisfaction of need. The user does not know the resources or information resources needed to satisfy the need when they begin a search session. In fact the searcher may not even know the true information need until they have learned from the resources encountered in searching and browsing.

6.2.10   BASIC LEVEL CATEGORIES

The Basic Level Category (BLC) concept was first developed by Rosch (1973) and is further explained in Lakeoff's book *Woman, Fire and Dangerous Things* (2008). Donna Mauer, an Australian IA researcher, summarized the BLC concept as follows (2006).

- Categories are organized from most general to most specific. But there is a *basic level* somewhere in the middle of a hierarchy.

- This cognitively basic level is learned the earliest, usually has a short name, and is used frequently.

- Basic levels are the highest level at which a single mental image can reflect a category.

- Most of our knowledge is organized around basic level categories.

Mauer also made suggestions to make best uses of BLCs in IA design:

- When organizing the site structure, we can work from the middle out by starting with basic levels of categorization.

- Basic levels have a good information scent because they can be identified quickly (short and frequently utilized). They make good "trigger" words to help people choose their information path.

- Try getting people to the basic level of the hierarchy as soon as possible.

For IAs working with tags and social classification, you may ask the question: Are tags at the basic level? If yes, they might have natural advantages over their counterparts in a taxonomy or controlled vocabulary.

6.2.11 THEORIES SUMMARY

The theories above represent some of the ways academics distilled empirical data into characterizations of HIB information spaces, representing within the mind, social or psychological, and behavioral concepts. All have a relation, of varying degrees, to information system design. In addition to the academic theories above, interaction design has its own set of guidelines and principles, which we will discuss in following chapters.

6.3   DESIGN IMPLICATIONS

Our knowledge about human information behavior informs the design to better meet the user needs and minimize user frustration. Here are some general design guidelines.

- Create structure and navigation to meet users' mental model and expectations.

- Design to support quick scanning and strong information scent.

- Help people know what they don't know, combat the "Principle of Least Effort."

- Set up the right default settings.

- Allow people time for decision-making and motivate people to complete transactions, for example by:

    ○ narrowing down options and supporting easy comparison between objects;

    ○ saving unfinished shopping carts for users between sessions in eCommerce environments; and

    ○ showing actual number of items remaining in lists, like search results or in large easily browsed collections.

6.3.1   WEB USE CONSIDERATIONS

Because the web is such an important part of the information landscape, we share several IA considerations for web design and search below. Long before the invention of the web information scientists and HCI researchers started studying user information behavior. The growth of the web, however, made the user population "explode" quickly and created additional usage patterns as well. The following patterns are summarized based on the studies at different times in various contexts. Note most of these findings were more focused on non-repeated uses of public websites. Some of them may not be completely applicable to frequent and expert users of a website.

6.3.2   WEB USERS DON'T READ PAGES, THEY SCAN

Much of web use is motivated by the desire to quickly find information. As a result, web users tend to act like sharks: they have to keep moving, or they'll die. Users just don't have the time or patience to read any more than necessary.

Nielsen's eye tracking study with 200+ web users identified a strong "F" shaped reading pattern (2006). Users first read in a horizontal movement, usually across the upper part of the content area. This initial element forms the F's top bar. Next, users move down the page a bit and then read across in a second horizontal movement that typically covers a shorter area than the previous movement. This additional element forms the F's lower bar. Finally, users scan the content's left side in a vertical movement (Figure 6.1).

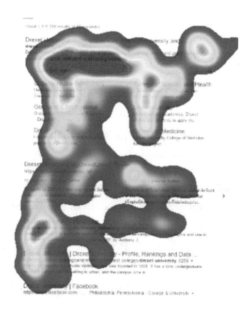

Figure 6.1: The "F" shaped reading pattern, observed with eye-tracking tools in one of the author's studies.

6.3.3   WEB USERS DON'T MAKE OPTIMAL CHOICES, THEY SATISFICE

Satisficing is seeking information that is *good enough*. Unlike the general rational decision-making model, which includes identifying a problem, gathering information, identifying the possible solutions, and choosing the best one (sometimes called "optimizing" or "maximizing") web users are often in a hurry and tend to adopt a satisficing model. However, satisficing behavior is still often used by people like firefighters, pilots, chess masters, and nuclear power plant operators (Krug, 2005). These people make high-stakes decisions in real settings with time pressure, vague goals, limited information, and changing conditions. They do not compare options. Instead they take the first reasonable plan that comes to mind and do a quick mental test for problems. If they do not find any, they have their plan of action. Compare this to maximizing, where large amounts of information are carefully considered before making a decision.

In addition, there's usually not much of a penalty for guessing wrong in the web environment; weighing options may not improve the chances, guessing is more fun, and the penalty is low for guessing wrong—usually just a click of the back button.

6.3.4   HOW DO PEOPLE SEARCH THE WEB?

Here is a summary of findings about how people search on the web.

- Number of search words per query: 2–3 words.

- People do not often use advanced search features.

- Public queries are often short, not much modified, and simple in structure (Spink and Jansen, 2004).

- People examine eight search results on average; a majority of users only examined the first five (Nielsen and Loranger, 2006).

- Short search sessions: Spink and Cole (2006), based on search log analysis, report "A substantial percentage of web sessions are less than 5 minutes. Searchers do not appear willing to go to the second or three results pages. Typical users view an average of 8 web documents per session. A significant % of web search engine users, however, view no more than 5 web documents per session. Typically, a web searcher will spend about 5 minutes or less evaluating a web document, with almost 15% spending less than 30 seconds."

- People do not usually go past the first page of results. Nielsen and Loranger (2006) reported the following: Only the first search engine results page (SERP) was visited in 93% of searches; users got to the second SERP in 7% of the searches, among which 5% of users actually clicked the links. Only 47% of users scrolled down on the first SERP.

Design for Search Systems

Users browse by following links and search to find information. Marti Hearst's book, *Search User Interfaces* (2009), is a good resource for deeply exploring search. For our purposes, search is one of many IA components that work together to make the website/application as a whole to achieve much higher performance than the sum of the individual systems. When designing a search interface, the following issues need to be considered.

- **How long should the search box be?** Do long queries lead to better search results? Longer search boxes invite more search terms, however, long natural language searches may not be better. When the number of search terms reaches a certain threshold, the number of search results drops dramatically and it does not guarantee most relevant results. Madden, et. al. (2007) concluded the "best search strategy is a combination of simplicity and scrutiny." Encouraging interactive searches and letting the users pick more keywords from the relevant results seems to be more helpful and effective.

- **How many search boxes are needed?** Sometimes multiple search boxes can appear in an interface. The screenshot below shows an interface with both website and people directory (phone book) search boxes on the intranet of Drexel University. Which one is better, one search box or multiple? One search box is almost always better. With faceted search and sorting, multiple search boxes can be combined.

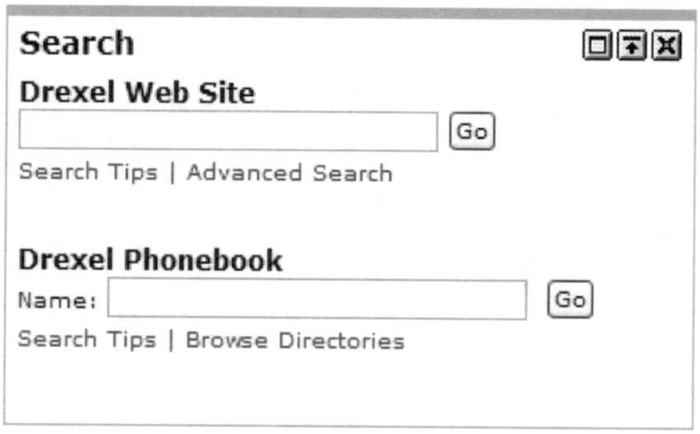

Search   □ ⊞ ⊠

Drexel Web Site

[   ] [Go]

Search Tips | Advanced Search

Drexel Phonebook

Name: [   ] [Go]

Search Tips | Browse Directories

Figure 6.2: Intranet site with two search boxes.

- **Should we provide search assistance/shortcuts?** Search assistance, such as: auto-complete/typeahead, spell checking, stemming, search histories, and thesaurus searching can be very helpful to the user. The common "did you mean" feature which corrects spelling is a good example of assistance.

- **Should we design for advanced search?** Given that only a small number of people use advanced search features, keyword search should be the default. Advanced search may be made available via a link or other control, but do not count on people using it.

- **How to display meaningful search results?** When the search is against multiple sources, the search results can be displayed corresponding to the source/type, such as Google showing tabs for images, news, and video. Or the results can be combined together in one list with visual cues to indicate the type of result. Faceted search with filters and sorting helps users drill down to meaningful results. Sorting also supports exploration of search results. Additionally, showing the query term highlighted in results summaries can be helpful.

6.4   SUMMARY

Information behavior theories can be very helpful in providing guidance and background for design. Research from several areas has provided insights into human behaviors we see in information spaces that can inform design decisions. However, theory cannot solve all your design problems. IAs and user researchers need to weigh in with their own findings based on user research in context, as well as using theory, principles, and guidelines. Theories have implications on design, the web in particular is a good place to explore when looking for examples of HIB's impact on IA.

CHAPTER 7

Interaction Design

The Interaction Design Association defined Interaction Design as follows (2009):

> *Interaction design (IxD) is the branch of User Experience Design that illuminates the relationship between people and the interactive products they use. While Interaction Design has a firm foundation in the theory, practice, and methodology of traditional user interface design, its focus is on defining the complex dialogues that occur between people and interactive devices of many types—from computers to mobile communications devices to appliances.*

IxD is a broad concept, emphasizing the interaction between people and the interface. Established as a discipline with different concerns and foci, IxD emerged from traditional User Interface Design (aka "man-machine interaction" or "human-computer interaction"), while IA was driven by the need for information organization. The former is more concerned about the user's control and the systems response, and the latter emphasizes the connections between information elements and related functionalities. However, in our highly connected information societies IA and IxD are more and more intertwined, and the overlap between the two is getting stronger. The interaction design we discuss here is mainly focused on the overlapping areas (Figure 7.1).

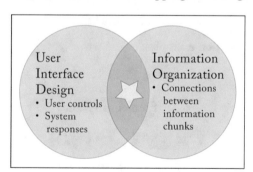

Figure 7.1: Intersection of UI design and information organization.

Just like information architecture work existed before the IA discipline was established, IxD started way before the web and mobile were invented. Interaction design exists in desktop applications, handhelds, kiosks, TV-based interfaces, automotive interfaces, appliances, audible interfaces, and many more. This chapter uses examples from the web, as web interfaces are a common ground we all share and are applicable to many domains.

7.1   INTERACTION DESIGN PRINCIPLES

Interaction design principles come at multiple levels. Cooper (2004) categorized them into four levels: *Design values, conceptual principles, behavioral principles,* and *interface level principles.* The design principles we focus on in this chapter are grounded in the theories we've discussed, and are mainly at the behavioral and interface level.

7.1.1   FITT'S LAW: DESIGN FOR FITT'S

Fitt's Law maintains that the time required to move rapidly from a starting point to a final target area is a function of the distance to the target and the size of the target. Therefore, it is better to put targets closer to where they are likely to be used (e.g., put buttons next to the activities they relate to), and to make them larger.

To summarize, Fitt's Law tells us when designing an actionable object on the page (e.g., buttons or links).

- **Bigger is better:** Important functions should be presented with large objects/buttons.

- **Closer is faster:** Contextual action buttons or links should be presented within reasonable proximity.

- **Less fine motor control is required:** Correspondingly, when the target is so small or surrounded so closely by other objects, the user will have to slow down the pace to choose very carefully in order to avoid misclicks.

Let's look at some pagination examples:

page 1 | 2 | 3 | 4 | 5 | 6

(from eluxury.com)

< Back 1 2 3 Next >

(from washingtonpost.com)

1 2 3 4 5 6 7 8 9 10 Next »

(from shopping.yahoo.com)

Which design above do you think is easier to click? You may think the answer is a no brainer, but it really reflects Fitt's Law—bigger is better. The design with larger clickable areas wins. The final design makes the square area surrounding the number clickable, which is easier to do than just clicking on the number itself.

Here is another set of examples using a Microsoft toolbar.

This shows the toolbar of icons without text labels.

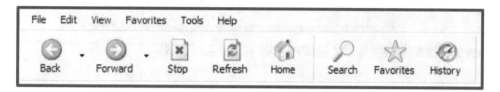

This shows the same toolbar of icons and text labels.

Which one is easier? For many people the buttons that have both text and icons are easier to hit because the clickable areas are bigger (let alone labels reduce ambiguity of the icons). In addition, each button is more spread out, which reduces the possibility of clicking on the wrong button by accident. Especially for people with motor disabilities, Fitt's Law can help reduce errors by providing larger targets.

Corners and Edges

IAs should also take advantage of corners and edges for better Fitt's. These areas are "infinitely targetable" and require less fine motor control because of the boundary created by the edges of the screen. As a user moves their cursor, they cannot go "past" the boundary of the screen, so the cursor stops there no matter how much more the user moves their mouse in that direction. Of course, with touchscreens we don't see this behavior so it is limited to desktop/mouse interfaces.

Compare the designs of the Start button in older versions of Microsoft Windows (Figure 7.2). Which one gives better Fitt's? The Start button had a single "dead" pixel along the left and bottom sides of it in which clicking didn't open the Start menu. From a usability perspective the pixel resulted in lower acquisition times and a large number of misclicks. With the second design, the clickable area for the "start" menu is much bigger, and also due to the elimination of a single pixel, it gained infinite Fitt's.

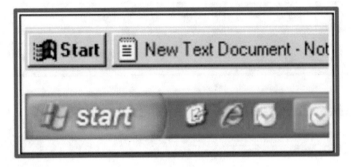

Figure 7.2: Different versions of the Windows Start menu.

7.1.2   DESIGN FOR AFFORDANCE

An affordance points toward whatever action can be taken using an object. Good affordances have *"strong visual clues to the operation of things"* (Norman, 1998). For example, a chair affords sitting, a button affords pushing, and a handle may afford turning or pulling. Norman's insight was that perceived affordances are even more important than real affordances in terms of usability. An affordance is only as effective as it is perceivable. In order to ensure perceived affordance the design should meet user expectations, for example by following design conventions.

Affordances can be tricky to design in information spaces because all users are different. Cultural and other factors influence whether or not the user recognizes an affordance. There is a bit of an art and a science to it. At the same time, make sure non-actionable objects don't have an affordance. Explicit affordance (like text buttons) or implicit affordance (visual cues or context) can be used together to reinforce each other.

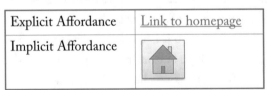

What are good ways to communicate affordances? Shape, color, and font are all ways we do that in information spaces. Location (words and icons in the header of an app often are menu links), grouping actionable items together (Hick's Law), and using metaphors (a shopping cart in eCommerce) are also good ways to communicate affordances.

7.1.3   DESIGN FOR EFFICIENCY

Efficiency allows the user to accomplish the task quickly. Simply put, make it easier and faster for users to complete tasks. Bruce Tognazzini (2001) discusses different ways to ensure efficiency, including decreasing data entry and limiting decision making on the user's side. To decrease data entry, the system can auto-fill information for the user based on previous user activities (Figure 7.3). Suggesting allowable data ranges or using selections can also save users time and prevent errors. To limit decision making by the user, the system should only present applicable choices (instead of presenting everything and then showing errors after the user selects invalid ones).

Figure 7.3: Typeahead functionality saves time and reduces error (misspellings).

7.1.4   DESIGN FOR FORGIVENESS

Forgiveness allows the user to feel less anxiety about making mistakes, and allows for imperfections in human activity. Don Norman (1998) provides a categorization of errors: capture errors, description errors, data-driven errors, associative activation errors, loss-of-activation errors, and mode errors. A perfect match does not exist between humans and computers; errors will occur and IAs must prevent "dead ends" in a system. There are different ways IAs can help.

Easy Reversal of Actions

Human beings make unintentional mistakes in many situations—we may be in a rush, under stress, or simply misunderstand what to do. Sometimes we just do something wrong or miss a target, clicking close when we intended something else. Easy reversal of actions protects users from being penalized by mistakes. The system should help users recover, be it an "are you sure" dialog, or even a "back" button on the web.

IAs must balance the reversal of actions with efficiency, evaluating the damage done if the action is not reversible versus the need for efficiency. In Figure 7.4, most times the user may be okay closing without saving changes—and indeed may want to do that. However, that one time in a hundred—where the student clicks "X" to close without saving the term paper (or even clicks close by accident)—can have serious consequences. So designers introduce a little inefficiency in order to prevent a potential catastrophe.

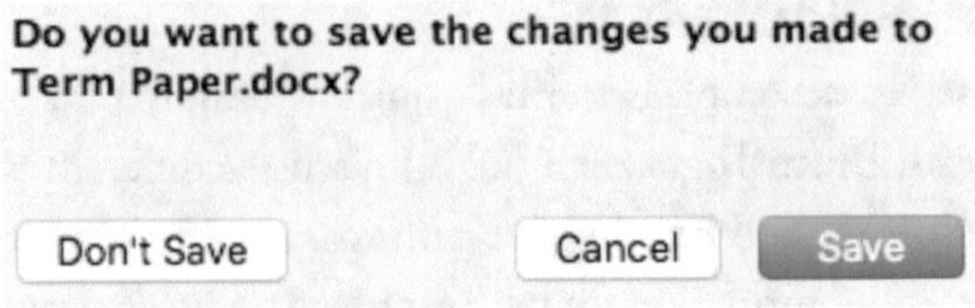

Do you want to save the changes you made to Term Paper.docx?

Don't Save   Cancel   Save

Figure 7.4: Dialog box preventing a potential catastrophic error.

Error Prevention

Designers should predict common problems and try to prevent them from happening. For example, data entry can be minimized and, therefore, the error rate can be minimized when menu selection is offered rather than free form text. Also, it is helpful to instruct the user upfront about certain rules (for example, in password creation). When errors cannot be completely avoided, try to isolate them as much as possible. One of the benefits of wizards is to help the user fix the problems that occurred in the current step so that they won't lead to more mistakes in many more subsequent steps for the whole process.

Error Handling

Error handling is the final step in dealing with errors. Error messages should be written to help the user detect the error and offer simple, constructive, and specific instructions for recovery.

7.1.5   DESIGN FOR USER PERCEPTIONS

User perceptions are not always right. Data collected in user research based on user perceptions (what they think or say) cannot be directly used to inform the design: researchers and designers must interpret these data. The things users think/say that happen could be quite different from what actually happens. Secondly, designing engaging experiences for users that reduce anxiety can dramatically increase user satisfaction. The story below is cited from Tognazzini's paper (2001).

> A classic example occurred in the 1930s in New York City, where "users" in a large new high-rise office building consistently complained about the wait times at the elevators. Engineers consulted concluded that there was no way to either speed up the elevators or to increase the number or capacity of the elevators. A designer was then called in, and he was able to solve the problem.

> What the designer understood was that the real problem was not that wait time was too long, but that the wait time was perceived as too long. The designer solved the perception problem by placing floor-to-ceiling mirrors all around the elevator lobbies.

People now engaged in looking at themselves and in surreptitiously looking at others, through the bounce off multiple mirrors. Their minds were fully occupied and time flew by.

When it comes to time, user perception can be wrong. For example, in one of Tognazzini's studies every user was able to perform a task using the mouse significantly faster than keyboard. However, all of the users reported completing the task much faster using the keyboard. In addition, it is very important to reduce the "subjective" or "perceived" system response time when it cannot really be shortened. He recommends a strategy to keep users engaged, and offers tactics for reducing the subjective experience of system "down time." We often see these types of techniques used to show progress status, like a spinning "loading" icon which helps make the wait time less boring and more tolerable.

7.1.6   DESIGN FOR HELP

The best "help" is to make the design intuitive enough so that people do not need help and the UI requires no explanation. Why? We know, based on the least effort principle, only a small number of people will read help documents; we also know people often muddle through difficult systems. Using help slows people down and takes them out of their task flow. They are not interested in learning about the system; they want to complete a task and achieve a goal.

However, sometimes help will still be needed. Because people naturally learn best while doing, it is often more useful and effective to provide help in the context of the user task. For example, displaying specific instructions when the mouse cursor is in the data field so that the user can adjust their input based on the instructions (see Figure 7.5).

Figure 7.5: Microsoft's user sign up form.

7.1.7   DESIGN FOR COLOR BLINDNESS

Approximately 8% of human males and 0.5% of females in North America have some form of color blindness, and red-green color deficiency is most common. Therefore, clear cues should be used in addition to color in order convey information in the interface, for those who are color-blind.

Do not rely solely on color to communicate meaning. For example, online forms may present an error message for invalid input. Commonly, red is used to highlight errors. If the original form uses green for field labels, and red for highlighting errors, people red-green color blindness will not see a difference. In cases like this, add an icon in front of the data field or use some other mechanism to convey the invalid message. Always use a non-color way of communicating meaning.

Take a look at traffic signs in the physical world (Figure 7.6). Besides color, they also use shapes to convey the information. Instantly we know that on the left, the sign means to stop. Try to use similar ideas in your designs.

Figure 7.6: Traffic signs.

7.1.8   DESIGN FOR PERSONALIZATION AND CUSTOMIZATION

Personalization and customization are now commonly seen in many online spaces like eCommerce and intranet sites. While the two are closely related and sometimes used interchangeably, we differentiate them for our discussion.

- **Personalization** is a systematically generated view of the user's own information based on user attributes or activities in the past.

- **Customization** allows the user to make manual changes, and adjust the look and feel, navigation, and content.

Personalization based on the history of actual user activities is more reliable than personalization based on voluntary self-reported data (e.g., demographics, preferences, and interests). Personalized information should be carefully created and presented. Many eCommerce sites take a personalization approach by making user-activity-based recommendations (e.g., past purchase history). In the business intranet environment, personalization can be based on job function, role, and many other detailed HR data points. While the non-personalized versions contain content for everyone, the personalized version starts to show more targeted interfaces.

Customization allows the user to choose what to see and when they want to see it. The challenges are clear: It is hard to determine how much control is enough for the user—too much control can easily become overwhelming. In addition, while the user needs change dynamically, it is not guaranteed that customization can always match the user needs, let alone meet real user needs. Finally, the designer still needs to design default views, given the notoriously low customization rate by the end user.

While appropriately designed personalization and customization help improve information relevance and can build user loyalty, they cannot eliminate the need to design a good default site structure and navigation. Furthermore, even the personalized areas require good information architecture and navigation.

7.2   INTERACTION DESIGN COMPONENTS

7.2.1   VIEWS, FORMS, AND WORKFLOW

Views are web pages used for information viewing and navigation; *forms* are used for data creation, editing, and submission. The controls on the page, such as links, buttons, icons, and selection devices, allow the user to conduct the interaction with the system, such as submit or request data. When different views and forms are combined together to support a certain user task, they become a *workflow*. There are different types of workflows: hubs, wizards, and guides (the combination of hubs and wizards). Hubs (Figure 7.7) are used when there is a primary view page containing a collection of data elements and a series of one-page forms for editing the elements. Hubs are found in a variety of applications, such as calendars and email. Usually, there is no dependency among the (sub) tasks (forms) in the hub structure.

Wizards, also called serial processes, are made up of a sequence of forms linked with "Previous (back)" and "Next (continue)" buttons. Wizards require users to fill out forms one at a time, navigating through the process in a predetermined fixed sequence (shown in Figure 7.8). After completing all the forms in the sequence, the user is typically taken to a view page summarizing the choices. Typically, the "Shopping cart checking out" process on eCommerce sites takes a wizard approach. It is commonly used for desktop software installation as well. The wizards approach breaks the complex user tasks into multiple simple steps and guides the user through the process.

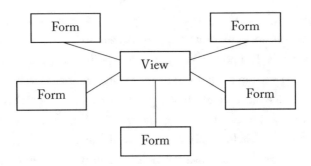

Figure 7.7: Hub structure.

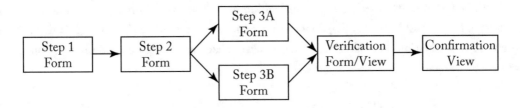

Figure 7.8: Wizard structure.

7.2.2 FILTERS AND CONTROLS

Filters and controls are the devices available on web pages for the user to interact with the system. There are many types, including drag and drop, zoom in/out, sliders, buttons, links, checkboxes, expand and collapse, tabs, selection devices, search and filter, auto-complete, and date picker. On the web, sometimes clicking on a control in a web page navigates to a new page, or sometimes it controls a function that remains on the current page. With dynamic technologies, such as Javascript and CSS, web interactions continue to get more and more dynamic and responsive. Users should be made aware of the control's action as much as possible, so they can predict its behavior.

7.2.3 INTERACTIVITY

The websites we see today commonly use a technology called "AJAX"—a term coined by a well known information architect, Jessie James Garrett (2005). AJAX is short for "Asynchronous Javascript And XML." This technology allows parts of a web page to refresh, sending and receiving data to and from a server, without the need for the entire page to reload. All project team members should understand the implications of interactions, including:

- the need to make options and affordances immediately evident (e.g., drag-and-drop);

- be aware of subtle changes on the page that users don't notice;

- provide a clear task flow ("what do I do next?");

- be aware of requiring fine motor skills to manipulate the interface, and increasing disruptive user errors;

- do not overload users with too much information and unnecessary visual complexity; and

- evaluate for accessibility concerns (connection speed, ADA/Section 508 Compliance).

While these interaction design examples we use in this chapter are geared toward the web, they are applicable to almost any interactive systems. An automobile dashboard interface, for example, is likely to follow the hub/wizard structures, and adhere to the interactivity implications presented above.

7.3   SUMMARY

Interaction design is about the intersection of users, interfaces, and information. IAs are often called upon to design interactive interfaces. At the very least, IA work (even if just on the back end content and metadata) will have an impact on the user interface. Several principles have come about over the years that can be used (often alongside other principles and theories) to help guide interaction design. IAs can look to examples on the web for help identifying components they might use in any information system, be it web based or otherwise.

CHAPTER 8

Design Patterns, Emerging Principles, and Mobile Considerations

Design patterns and principles help IAs create new information spaces that remain consistent with previous systems, leveraging users' learned behaviors and experiences. This chapter introduces design patterns and emerging principles used today in IA, UX, and related fields. We use the popular Bootstrap framework to illustrate how patterns can be used and reused across information spaces to provide familiar interfaces for users. Similarly, emerging principles like responsive design guide IAs toward designing effective information spaces today and for the future. Finally, we look at the mobile space.

8.1 DESIGN PATTERNS

The idea of patterns in information sciences largely comes from the influential architect and theorist Christopher Alexander, who described a "pattern language" for architecture. Patterns provide us the tools and framework for creating meaningful, functional, and beautiful architectures: they are the starting points for design. Architects use patterns by first examining the context of each space:

> To make the building live, its patterns must be generated on site, so that each one takes its own shape according to its context.—Christopher Alexander (1979)

Alexander had thousands of years of building and architecture from which to draw his patterns, while IAs have had just a few dozen years. Nevertheless, some patterns are used across many different types of information spaces. You are probably familiar with many of them from using websites and apps, like websites having a footer and header. The benefits of using patterns include (Gerchev, 2012):

- accelerated process, by reusing components;

- proven solutions, and increased confidence in the design;

- encourages consistency;

- supports communication among team members by using a shared language;

- novice IAs can utilize proven components; and

- patterns are familiar to users, supporting affordances because the user has experience and learned from them before.

8.1.1 CRITICISM OF PATTERNS

It may be discouraging to think about patterns, on the assumption that IAs must follow that which has come before. Is IA just copying what already exists? Is it really the case that "consistency is the curse of innovation in design" (Budiu, 2016)? We answer these questions with a resounding "no!"

Remember, information architecture is an art and science. Part of the art is using, reusing, and mashing up patterns and principles into something new. Returning to Alexander's work, think about the thousands of years of history in architecture. If patterns truly are a curse than we would see nothing new, yet every year exciting buildings are constructed that inspire and amaze. Successfully using patterns and principles is more than copying what you've seen in the past; it is creating something new, based on the foundations of what has come before. Think of patterns like the ingredients in a recipe; by combining them in different ways you can get radically different outcomes, even when others have the same ingredients.

8.1.2 PATTERNS AND INNOVATION

Patterns "may be a reasonable starting point, but they are only a starting point. The value in UI consistency lies in effective learning, by making it easy to transfer knowledge from another product without interfering with ease of use." (Microsoft, n.d.-a)

Patterns help innovation by providing users a way to transfer skills they've learned in their experiences with previous systems. This helps with adoption—people will more likely try and use a technology where they have some intuitive sense of how it works. Additionally, they will reach proficiency more quickly than if they had to learn the system from the ground up. Apple for example has a long history of creating hardware, software, and apps that "just work," and they also have a long history of creating detailed design standards for others to follow (Apple Computer Inc, 1993).

Examining Apple's and others' design documentation reveals a truism of IA: *It's very hard to make a design seem effortless.* Balancing the new and old is challenging. Apple's patterns when creating new products like the iPhone were built on established ideas in information architecture, software design, and the web. With some grounding in what had come before, entirely new interactions and devices were born that delighted users.

8.1.3 DESIGN PATTERN EXAMPLES

Below we share two design pattern examples, from Bootstrap and the Yahoo! developer network. The former is more logical (meaning closer to pixel perfect design), while the latter includes more conceptual elements. These are just two of the many pattern libraries available for IAs to browse and draw inspiration.

Bootstrap

Bootstrap is a popular HTML, CSS, and JavaScript framework used to develop responsive websites and apps. The framework was originally developed at Twitter, and is now "open-source," meaning anyone can use it for his or her projects. Thousands of websites today use this framework as a foundation to jumpstart their design and development, because it includes many common elements that most designers and developers need in their designs like buttons, search boxes, and more. Below are some examples that should be familiar to you, which were created by an IA in minutes using code from the Boostrap website: http://getbootstrap.com/about/. By selecting from the "ingredients" Bootstrap provides, IAs can quickly gather what they need to "cook" great designs.

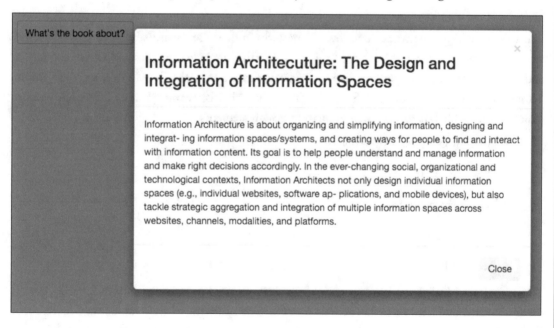

Figure 8.1: Bootstrap modal element.

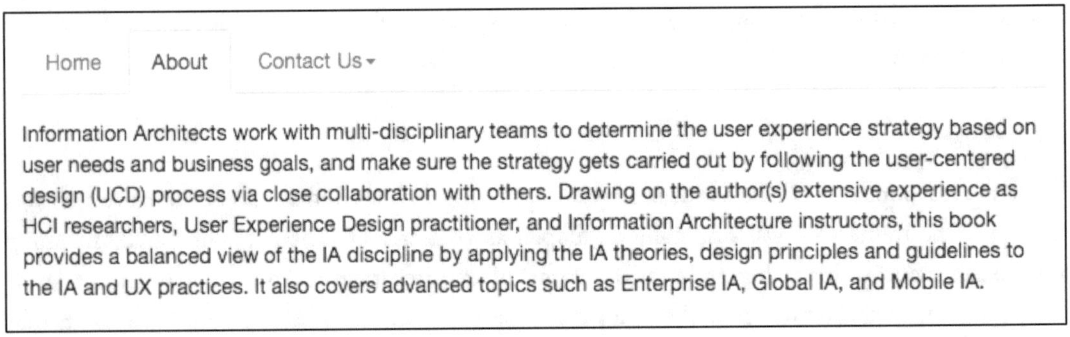

Home	About	Contact Us ▾

Information Architects work with multi-disciplinary teams to determine the user experience strategy based on user needs and business goals, and make sure the strategy gets carried out by following the user-centered design (UCD) process via close collaboration with others. Drawing on the author(s) extensive experience as HCI researchers, User Experience Design practitioner, and Information Architecture instructors, this book provides a balanced view of the IA discipline by applying the IA theories, design principles and guidelines to the IA and UX practices. It also covers advanced topics such as Enterprise IA, Global IA, and Mobile IA.

Figure 8.2: Bootstrap tabs element.

Yahoo! Design Patterns

The Yahoo! developer network shares over 50 patterns in their library, available at https://developer.yahoo.com/ypatterns/everything.html (Yahoo!, n.d.). They include examples and advice about how and when to use common patterns like Calendar Pickers, Carousels, Tag Clouds, and many more. To help designers use patterns effectively, Yahoo! lists the following questions for each pattern, which are good for IAs to ask when evaluating design elements.

- What problem does this solve?

- When to use this pattern

- What's the solution?

- Why use this pattern?

- Accessibility.

Over time individual IAs and entire organizations tend to build up pattern libraries, even if on an informal basis. It just makes sense: users recognize patterns so they can operate more effectively (recognition over recall), and patterns speed up projects because design elements and the corresponding code can be re-used. A powerful technique when communicating complex interactivity from design to development is to "show don't tell," meaning find examples of the live interaction and provide that for the software developers. As patterns are used over and over, they both influence and are influenced by the topic of our next section, emerging principles.

8.2   EMERGING PRINCIPLES

The best designers sometimes disregard the principles of design. When they do so, however, there is usually some compensating merit attained at the cost of the violation. Unless you are certain of doing as well, it is best to abide by the principles (Lidwell et al., 2003).

We've looked at established theories, guidelines, and principles in past chapters. Here, we discuss "emerging principles," that come from interactive interfaces in the integrated era (Chapter 1). Like patterns, they help ensure that users can move within and between information spaces, effectively and efficiently accomplishing their goals with a high degree of understanding.

Because technology changes so fast and design is constantly evolving, we use the label "emerging" principles, as they will evolve over time. One important way to remain ahead of fast changing technology is to create information spaces that can adapt without the need for costly redesigns. Responsive design is an example of a principle that helps us "respond" to new technology.

8.2.1   RESPONSIVE DESIGN

Responsive design is a way to serve multiple devices at once, without creating unique websites or apps for each. Rather than design and develop for desktop and smartphone, responsive design means we have one codebase (HTML, CSS, JavaScript, etc.) that serves all devices. Some design teams even take a "mobile first" strategy and create for mobile as the primary target, with larger screens secondary, recognizing the sustained importance of mobile devices.

"Breakpoints" define screen resolutions in a responsive design framework, where the layout will change for different sized screens. A good way to find useful breakpoints for a project is to examine web logs for screen resolutions, and set breakpoints at the most common sizes for mobile, tablet, desktop, and super-large. Examining web logs can tell the IA which screen sizes and devices are most valuable for the design.

8.2.2   GRIDS

Responsive design relies on "grids," which are columns and rows in which elements are placed. As the screen size changes breakpoints are triggered; each "container" in the grid is moved to a location specified by the designer. Figures 8.3 and 8.4 show a simple eight-column grid layout that then adapts to a smaller screen with a four-column grid layout. Containers may be more than one column wide, for example the Main.Body container is six columns wide in Figure 8.3, and four wide in Figure 8.4.

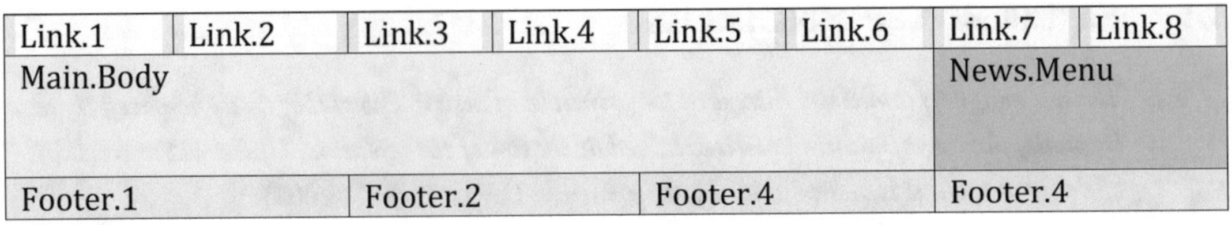

Link.1	Link.2	Link.3	Link.4	Link.5	Link.6	Link.7	Link.8
Main.Body						News.Menu	
Footer.1		Footer.2		Footer.4		Footer.4	

Figure 8.3: Example page grid. The top row shows eight containers which can hold header navigation links. Row 2 shows main body, and a news menu on the right. The last row contains footer text and links. As the page resizes, each container in the grid can adapt to the new screen size.

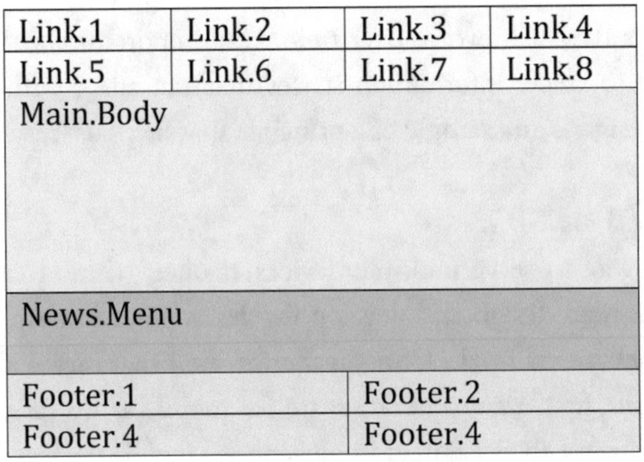

Link.1	Link.2	Link.3	Link.4
Link.5	Link.6	Link.7	Link.8
Main.Body			
News.Menu			
Footer.1		Footer.2	
Footer.4		Footer.4	

Figure 8.4: The grid elements as above, reorganized for a narrower screen.

We think about responsive design and grids like this: each container should be independent. When the screen size changes, the containers will be rearranged. IAs help decide at what screen resolution these breakpoints are set and come up with ideas for how the content will display. Note that while the codebase may stay the same, saving development efforts, the IA will likely have to create design deliverables for each size screen identified for the system. Breakpoints are often set for:

- smartphones, vertical and horizontal;

- tablets, vertical and horizontal;

- medium laptops/desktops;

- large laptops/desktops; and

- very large desktops, multiple monitors, televisions.

Atomic Design

An interesting way to think about the designs is to look at them like atoms and molecules in chemistry. Brad Frost developed this idea into "Atomic Design," a principle that breaks down an interface into "atoms," then builds it back up to form "molecules, organisms, templates, and pages" (2016). Atomic design attempts to identify each individual element and use them to build bigger and bigger parts of a website. Using the chemistry analogy, Frost explains atomic design as follows: "The atoms of our interfaces serve as the foundational building blocks that comprise all our user interfaces. These atoms include basic HTML elements." Moving to the next level, "molecules are relatively simple groups of UI elements functioning together as a unit." Molecules go together to form organisms, which are "complex UI components." Moving away from the chemistry analogy, Frost goes on to explain that molecules can be put together to form templates and pages.

8.2.3   GENERAL PRINCIPLES FROM LEADING TECH COMPANIES

Leading technology companies like Apple, Google, and Microsoft have all published design guidelines for internal designers and outside designers who may create apps that work on their platforms (e.g., a startup that makes a new iOS app for sale in the app store). These principles help ensure consistency. Below we've listed principles from these organizations: Look for common themes, we expect you'll find several across the lists, and you should see some overlap with interaction design principles (Chapter 7), and user information behaviors (Chapter 6).

Apple Principles

Apple developed ten design guidelines for iOS developers to follow (2016).

- **Formatting Content:** Users should see primary content without zooming or scrolling horizontally.

- **Touch Controls:** Use elements designed for touch gestures.

- **Hit Targets:** Controls should be at least 44x44 pixels, so they may be accurately tapped with a finger.

- **Text Size:** Size should be at least 11 pixels, so it is legible without zooming.

- **Contrast:** There should be ample contrast between text and the backround color, so the text is legible.

- **Spacing:** Design letter spacing and line height for legibility.

- **High Resolution:** Supply images suitable for high resolution screens.

- **Distortion:** Display images at their original ratio.

- **Organization:** Arrange content so it is easy to read and controls are near what they modify.

- **Alignment:** Align content so information relations are exposed.

Google Principles

Google created design and usability principles for their "material" design framework, that is used across Google products and in Android apps (Google, n.d.-b, n.d.-a):

- **repeating** visual elements, structural grids, and spacing across platforms and screen sizes;

- **clear layouts:** clearly visible elements, sufficient contrast and size, a clear hierarchy of importance, key information discernable at a glance;

- **navigate:** give users confidence in knowing where they are in your app and what is important;

- **understand important tasks:** reinforce important information through multiple visual and textual cues. Use color, shape, text, and motion to communicate what is happening; and

- **access your app:** include appropriate content labeling to accommodate users who experience a text-only version of your app.

Microsoft Principles

Microsoft developed techniques to create "powerful and simple" systems (Microsoft, n.d.-b); we've excerpted some of the most relevant for IA.

- combine what should be combined;

- separate what should be separated;

- eliminate what can be eliminated;

- put the elements in the right place;

- use meaningful high-level combinations;

- make tasks discoverable and visible;

- use text that users understand; and

- use safe, secure, probable defaults.

Notice how much overlap there is between the lists. Recalling Nielsen's 10 heuristics from Chapter 4, how many of these principles are similar? Emerging principles also offer a useful "check" on over-enthusiastic/overly complex design, or making a change just for the sake of change (remember the "keep it simple" principle).

8.3 MOBILE IA CONSIDERATIONS

According to the Pew Research Center (2014), "three major technology revolutions" provide the foundation for the modern information space landscape: broadband, social, and mobile. Each has had a substantial impact on how people interact with information and connect with one another, the role of the internet in our lives, and the role of IA in daily life and society. Below we discuss mobile as it has most relevance to IA.

Mobile represents a paradigm shift for information technology, and by extension, IA. The mobile revolution "made any time-anywhere access to information a reality for the vast majority of Americans" (Pew Research Center, 2014). With a mobile device like a smartphone, and a wireless connection, people have an unlimited supply of information at their fingertips anytime and anywhere. Smartphones are used for many information interactions, like texting, checking social media, browsing websites, and sometimes even making phone (or voice) calls.

Mobile apps and sites both augment and replace the desktop computer. Many people live a "mobile first" lifestyle; access via mobile is either their primary or only means of access (Wroblewski, 2012). The convenience of mobile phones makes them the device of choice, even in instances where another more "capable" device is nearby. In a "second screen" scenario, users have a primary device, like a TV, and use mobile for social media or other reasons.

If you are reading this (e)book on a college campus or in a metropolitan area, take a 5-min break, but come right back! Walk around for a few minutes and observe the people around you. What did you find? People are everywhere with glowing devices in their hands, texting with friends, playing games, or even doing coursework. Some of them may even be staring at their phones while walking on the sidewalk or crossing the street. These "distracted walkers" are a sign of how pervasive (and addictive!) mobile devices can be. A study by the American Academy of Orthopaedic Surgeons reports 26% of people surveyed report being in a "distracted walking incident," and of those who were in an incident, 3% broke a bone (American Academy of Orthopaedic Surgeons, 2015). Quite a compelling report about the power of mobile!

8.3.1   SMARTPHONE CHARACTERISTICS

When we reference mobile, we are talking about smartphones. The smartphone is:

- **small:** users are unlikely to carry very large devices;

- **multi-purposed and ubiquitous**, combining hardware (like GPS) and software (native apps). Apps and accessories leverage the phone's cameras, speakers, and other components;

- **personal**, a device used by one person and not normally shared, except in some emerging markets;

- **always on**, always connected, allowing significant opportunity for ongoing event-driven user interaction;

- **simple authentication** procedure using a SIM (Subscriber Identity Module) registered with the network operator; the owner is thus unambiguously identifiable; and

- **battery powered**, and slower than top-tier broadband.

Smartphones also have the following advantages.

- **Location specific.** Smartphones allow people to access and interact with location-specific and context-specific info at the moment on the go to aid the immediate course of action. For example, finding a store or a restaurant nearby.

- **Immediacy.** Smartphones also provide the convenience to do things in the moment or at the last minute. Same-day hotel booking at one point made up 90% of the overall bookings on the mobile site of Marriott.com.

- **Monitoring real-time information** or checking dynamic information repeatedly. Smartphones are also well suited for quick status checking, which does not take complex actions or a long time and sometimes can be time-fillers, such as getting alerts about real-time stock quotes or social media updates, news, weather, or traffic information.

- **Convenient.** Because smartphones often right at hand, many users prefer to use them over desktop computers. Frequent locations for mobile device use is in the home or where users had access to a computer (Müller et al., 2015; Nylander et al., 2009). In other words, the mobile phone is not a mere backup solution for when there is no computer available, but a tool that often provides quicker and more convenient access than a computer.

- **Multi-screen/Second screen.** Users sometimes have another device active, and use their mobile phones for a secondary purpose like texting or social media. An example of this is people tweeting real-time reactions to a sporting event (Google, 2015).

- **Inexpensive.** Compared with other devices, a mobile phone can provide a wealth of technology as a relatively low cost, including connectivity. This is particularly important in developing countries where cost and lack of infrastructure is acute.

- **Adaptable.** The openness of platforms and app stores give developers easy access to features like GPS and stored profiles, allowing for powerful mashups.

8.3.2   FOCUS ON THE MOBILE CONTEXT

IAs should keep mobile's strengths and weaknesses in mind. We've often found ourselves confronted with "desktop" targeted projects, and had to advocate for a more balanced desktop/mobile or even mobile-first approach. In these instances reviewing web or usage logs can provide great insights for the correct strategies.

8.3.3   MINIMIZING THE NEED FOR TEXT ENTRY

Minimizing user free-form text entry to avoid unnecessary errors has been one of the classical usability best practices all along. However, it becomes critical with the mobile user experience. Mobile users are more likely to make mistakes (due to misspelling or mistyping) or take shortcuts. Mistyping is common, leading to reliance on auto-correct when typing.

Whenever appropriate, allowing users to input information by making selections instead of entering. Auto-complete or auto-suggest features are very useful; spelling corrections and abbreviations can help increase error tolerance. Whenever possible, the site or the mobile app should provide the following as well: smart default value based on location (such as zip code), user preferences, or history; easy deletion of field values; saving input values from previous sessions or other programs on the mobile phone. Voice input is also increasing in use, replacing typing on the keyboard.

8.3.4   PRIOTITIZE ESSENTIAL INFORMATION

Because of the limited screen size and resolution, making the best use of the screen real estate becomes critical. Compared to a desktop website, the navigation, widgets and page layout need to be presented more succinctly on the page for ease of use. Similar to the conventional website design, the most frequently used (usually higher level) information should be near the top, where it is most visible and accessible. As the user scans the screen from top to bottom, the information displayed should progress from general to specific and from high level to low level.

8.3.5   OTHER MOBILE USABILITY BEST PRACTICES

Since the cursor control and positioning mechanism for mobile phones are different, there are additional interesting design challenges. Actionable buttons and controls need to have good spacing. If the controls stay too close together, users must spend extra time and attention being careful where they tap, and they are more likely to tap the wrong element. A simple, easy-to-use user interface should sufficiently space controls and other user-interaction elements so that users can tap accurately with a minimum of effort.

Maintain consistency between the website, the mobile/responsive design, and native mobile application. That way, the user can easily apply what she learned from one channel to another without unnecessary relearning or confusion.

8.3.6   MOBILE AS THE PLATFORM

The number of standalone mobile apps today is reported to exceed two million in the Android and Apple stores (Statistica, 2016). Given the features and personal nature of smartphones, they have become a platform for a variety of uses beyond information use and seeking. In addition to GPS for location, most smartphones have built-in cameras and sensors like an accelerometer that measures tilt, motion, and gestures. These sensors can be accessed by mobile apps for a variety of purposes, including games and fitness tracking.

Integration with other devices is another interesting feature of smartphones for IA. An example is as a universal remote control for TV, other multimedia devices, and even for controlling room settings (e.g., heater/cooler, lighting, etc). By connecting over WiFi, Bluetooth, or the internet, smartphones can control almost any device. Several automobile companies now have features that allow a user to control functions like unlocking doors and lowering the windows from their phones.

8.3.7   USER'S IDENTITY AND WALLET

The user/owner of a smartphone can be uniquely identified, which makes them useful as the owner's identity or credit card. This opens the door for many exciting opportunities to explore mobile devices to their full potential, such as mobile ticketing, mobile payment, and location-based "check-ins."

Mobile ticketing enables customers to purchase, order, receive, and check tickets any time and anywhere. It makes the smartphone the ticket, which can be checked or scanned like a paper ticket. Mobile payment, like ApplePay, makes the smartphone function like a user's credit card. By tapping on or near field communications, the smartphone initiates payments using options the user has set up in a payment app. Similarly, the smartphone can serve as a customer check-in device. When the user is in a location, they can choose to check-in using an app, creating a notification that they are there.

8.3.8   MOBILE AND PERSONALIZATION

Smartphones are naturally suitable for personal information management (PIM), such as address book, emails, messages, and calendar. PIM features have become context and location sensitive. For example, if the user has "buy textbook from bookstore" in her to-do list, when she drives by the bookstore, the smartphone will display a reminder about the book. Another scenario is about a business traveler on a trip. When she pays a restaurant bill with the mobile device, there can be a prompt from the expense management system to ask whether the user wants to capture it for future travel expense reimbursement.

More importantly, the smartphones will continue to get smarter, patiently monitoring your personalized preferences, and delivering information based on a particular situation. For example, the Google maps app can deliver real-time, updated directions to a user as she is driving to her destination, suggesting alternate routes based on updated traffic conditions.

8.3.9   PRIVACY AND SECURITY ISSUES NEED TO BE ADDRESSED

As more and more activities move to smartphones, privacy and security concerns must be addressed accordingly. For example, social network applications or sites must let users control their online presence information and thus prevent others from locating them as desired. While there will be an enormous amount of personal mobile usage data captured by mobile operators and service providers, consumer data protection will become a critical and urgent topic to be taken care of collaboratively via legal, technological, and legislative venues.

In summary, smartphones are a highly personal extension of the individual, and have unique sociological and technological attributes—they are location aware, temporally situated, and socially connected. The successful user experience design takes advantage of these technology factors to bring value to both the user and the business.

8.4   SUMMARY

Patterns and principles seem so easy. Yet, despite decades of practice and research, many information spaces still get it wrong. We think it is because there is sometimes an idea to change for the sake of change, or a lack of awareness that one can build on established patterns to create innovative but still usable information spaces. Relying on the concepts and ideas shared in this chapter, and staying up to date with the latest design patterns and principles (while contributing to them?) helps IAs save time, delight users, and create evolutionary and revolutionary information spaces.

CHAPTER 9

IA in Practice

When discussing the UCD methodology, we touched on many aspects of the IA practice. In previous chapters, we also talked about the relationship between Information Architecture (IA) and Interaction Design (IxD) as the critical components of User Experience Design (UX). The focus here is about how IAs work with related disciplines on projects and create business value. We discuss three related topics: Design Teams, Design and Development Frameworks, and our own Research to Design Framework.

9.1 DESIGN AND DEVELOPMENT TEAMS

9.1.1 MAKEUP OF A USER EXPERIENCE DESIGN TEAM

In addition to consulting firms and agencies, more and more organizations now have in-house design teams; UX is a growing area. Depending on many factors, the staff doing UX design work may have different titles and form various team configurations. Here, we introduce a typical model—the design staff coexists in a multidisciplinary team, usually called the User Experience team. The team is usually made up of:

- user researchers;

- information architects (IAs);

- interaction designers (ID);

- visual designers;

- content strategists; and

- managers.

Figure 9.1 shows an example of typical UX team efforts, based on our own experience. Along the timeline (x-axis), each role is involved with a different pattern of effort (y-axis). In the case of specialized IA and ID roles, IAs tend to be involved in the earlier phase (visioning and conceptual design phases) while the ID picks up the work as it comes to the logical design phase all the way through documentation and post-design support. The IA and ID roles may be played by the same people on some UX teams.

The user researcher gets involved in the project in a peak and valley pattern. When it is the time to conduct the user research they have their peak time. Then they gradually taper off (valley) as others implement the findings. When a conceptual design is completed and ready for usability testing, the user research peaks again. Another peak time occurs when the time comes to test a logical design prototype. The involvement of visual designers follows a different peak/valley pattern, with more involvement as IA efforts wind down.

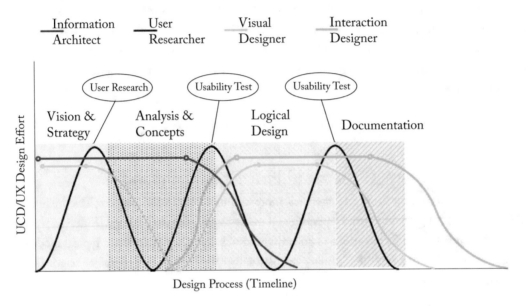

Figure 9.1: User experience design disciplines in the UCD process. The process may be iterative, with designs revisited due to findings from research/usability testing.

9.1.2 SPECIALISTS, GENERALISTS, AND "T-SHAPED" PROFESSIONALS

In a past IA Summit presentation, Jared Spool (2006) talked about generalists and specialists based on different team models. Generalists are the same people wearing multiple hats on the UX team, while specialists focus on their own disciplines and collaborate with specialists from other disciplines. Large organizations, as the design teams mature, tend to support specialists for several reasons: One being each role requires a different set of skills, and two being some roles (e.g., user researchers) need to maintain a certain objectivity in assessing the design. We often use this analogy to describe the relationship between designers and researchers—if designers are attorneys, researchers should play a judge role. This does not mean that designers are intentionally biased, but somehow may make certain unconscious assumptions along the way. When specialists work together, seamless collaboration and communication is important to the success of the team.

"T-shaped" professionals are people skilled in many areas, like generalists, but also have a depth of expertise in one area, like specialists. T-shaped individuals have "boundary-crossing" (Spohrer, 2015) skill sets. An example of this would be an expert ID who also can conduct research studies and work with content, and maybe even knows some programming or scripting. While T-shaped individuals can perform many roles, an equally important contribution is their ability to communicate effectively across disciplines. The script-savvy designer can help developers turn designs in working code by "speaking their language." In our lectures, we've also mentioned how IAs need to work with business people. That's another potential "T" proficiency, understanding skills needed to succeed in business.

9.1.3   CENTRALIZED VS. DISTRIBUTED ORGANIZATIONAL MODELS

In large organizations, there could be multiple design teams supporting different business lines. What is the ideal organizational model for the design teams? There are four business models to our knowledge. In some companies, there is a centralized UX group composed of individual UX teams for each business line. The UX group stands between the IT department and the business groups. In other companies, each UX group is part of the IT group supporting each business line. The way the third model works is that each UX group is embedded within each business line. The fourth one is hybrid. There are pros and cons for each of the three models.

- **Model 1, Centralized:** The centralized model allows the UX department to be the "Big Picture" keeper for the organization and makes it easier to push for enterprise design standards and guidelines, as well as design pattern sharing and reuse. It minimizes the learning curve for users (with coherent/consistent user experience). In addition, it allows for easier collaboration (across business lines) and best practice sharing. The UX team as a whole can have a stronger voice and higher visibility.

- **Model 2, Distributed across IT departments:** This model allows each UX team to focus on specific needs of each business line and also allows easier vertical resource management (the UX team and the IT development teams report to the same division/department). However, it is very easy to create isolated "design islands," which can be barriers for cross-organizational collaboration. Team A may not know about Team B's work.

- **Model 3, Distributed across the business lines (similar to Model 2):** The only difference is design teams in Model 2 are more likely to have intimate technological knowledge.

- **Hybrid:** a combination of the above models.

How to choose the right model? It depends on many factors, such as the size and type of business, the communications process the business needs, and the competitive advantage in providing a stellar user experience. For small organizations, there may not be a sizable UX team. Outside consultants may take on much of the IA/UX efforts, or hybrid positions may be created, like a web developer who also handles UX tasks.

Maximizing the IA Impact

Because IA continues to be an evolving discipline, the value to the business may not be fully seen by some people. Therefore, selling IA is as important as creating successful IA designs. In almost every organization, IAs need to sell their ideas to people at different levels to justify their existence, demonstrate their value, and build up their reputation. In order to be successful, IAs need to pay attention to the following aspects.

- Understand the business model.

- Know your audience. You need to deal with different types of people including IT departments, business sponsors and stakeholders, and senior management (Figure 9.2). You need to understand their interests and needs and use their language when advocating for IA. For example, IT teams are interested in less rework and reusable code; business sponsors need to see how your designs are aligned with their business objectives. Senior managers and executives are ultimately interested in how UX will lower costs, increase sales, and improve employee productivity. You need to manage the HiPPOs (Highest-Paid Person's Opinions).

- Fight the right battle. Do not expect that you can change the world over night. Prioritize the things and allow people time to buy-in. Also, keep in mind, you are not fighting against people, you are fighting for the right way to do things. At the end of the day, you need to have friends outside of the UX teams and disciplines instead of enemies, which leads to the next bullet point:

- Work on early adopters of UCD methodology and usability in the IT and business areas. The early adopters can then become UX champions to help spread the word and advocate the value.

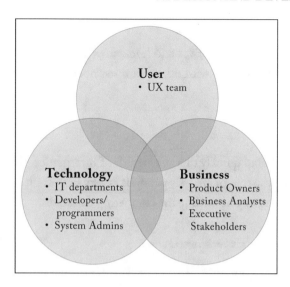

Figure 9.2: Teams and roles in the UCD process.

9.1.4   DESIRED COMPETENCIES AND SKILL SETS FOR IAS

For students who are interested in becoming information architects, the following qualifications are commonly seen in IA or related job descriptions. This is also what one of the authors required her team of IAs to have (Ding, 2009).

Being Strategic with Attention to Detail

Good IAs have the ability to work in great detail. But, at the same time, they can focus on broad strategic issues. The best information architects take user research, content analysis, business goals, and all of the other input information, and synthesize it into something that really works. They can see the big picture and keep an eye on all of the specific details.

Independent Thinker with Flexibility

Good IAs should demonstrate highly independent thinking. At the same time, they need to demonstrate flexibility to listen to others, be open to good ideas, and accommodate unpredictable needs.

Leader and Team Player

Any IA should be willing to take initiatives and leadership in any size or any type of effort. At the same time, they need to work closely with other team members and be willing to be a cooperative team player.

Problem Solver

A capable IA should be able to quickly digest a wealth of information thoroughly and make decisions effectively. Avoiding the trap of analysis paralysis is very important for anyone who is working in a fast-paced environment, or one with many competing demands.

Being Passionate About User Experience Design

Passion about user experience differentiates an excellent IA from a merely good IA.

Design Skills

Good IAs should be experts at converting user needs and business goals into appropriate designs. We consider this as the top competency of any good IAs. We would like once again to differentiate "user wants" and "user needs." Good IAs/designers listen to the user, diagnose the problem, and then provide solutions. It is risky to simply give what the user or the business sponsor wants. We don't want to underestimate the value of visual design, but it is important to know that the aesthetics alone cannot improve design effectiveness if the user needs are met. Visual design must be well integrated into the overall interaction flow.

And, of course, IAs should have in-depth knowledge in the following aspects we have covered earlier:

- information organization and information retrieval knowledge;

- HCI knowledge, including user cognitive characteristics and user behavior patterns;

- user research methods and usability engineering techniques;

- knowledge about UCD methodology and system development process; and

- communication, marketing, and project management skills.

9.2   DESIGN AND DEVELOPMENT FRAMEWORKS

As we've discussed, IAs work in teams with other disciplines. In order to manage projects, several frameworks have been developed to help people work together when creating information spaces.

For decades "Waterfall" was the only way to create software. Waterfall development favors heavy documentation, building to pre-established requirements, and delivering the final product at a predetermined deadline (which is often missed). We can easily see the problems with the waterfall approach: It does not incorporate change easily, which can mean delivering products that fail to meet rapidly changing user needs. To counter this, frameworks like Agile were created to help add flexibility in design and development. Below we present several frameworks that IAs are likely to encounter in practice.

9.2.1   AGILE

Agile software development began in 2001 with the Agile Manifesto (Figure 9.3), as a reaction to previous waterfall methods (Beck et al., 2001). Agile prioritizes incremental development, responses to changing priorities and technologies, and collaboration with users (called customers). Pivoting and changing direction as new information becomes available, while incrementally delivering features and functionality is fundamental. An important role in Agile teams is the "Product Owner," who is responsible for the overall vision of a product and prioritizes features for design and development, balancing the three components of user-centered design: Business, Technology, and Users. IAs and Product Owners work closely together.

Often Agile is practiced using a "scrum" process in which features are delivered at the end of relatively short "sprints." Sprints are development cycles typically lasting between one and four weeks. At the end of each sprint users are able to interact with the new features, affording IAs the opportunity to inspect the usability of a live system and plan changes for the next iteration. Another popular flavor is "Kanban," which focuses on work in progress, and is less structured than scrum.

In Agile scrum, there are a few points for IAs to consider.

- **Sprint 0:** This is the planning phase before development starts. Substantial user research often happens in this phase.

- **Sprint Ahead:** Because Agile sprints happen in time-bound segments, IAs often work one or two sprints ahead of developers, preparing wireframes and prototypes for them to code.

- **Demos:** These are the days where the final working features are demonstrated on the last day of the sprint. IAs can inspect how well the work was implemented, and plan any needed adjustments.

- **Spikes:** Agile comes from the software development world and is aimed at producing working code. Spike tasks are for research and information gathering activities, rather than producing code.

An important component of Agile that aligns well with IA/UX is the principle of "customer collaboration over contract negotiation," meaning collaborating with users (customers) to find what features should be built, over building only those features determined at the outset of a project. This is a big difference from waterfall in that the team can change course—the final product may be changed from what was first conceived. For example, let's say a library is creating a new website, and they learn that social book reviews are very important to their patrons, even though it was not a priority feature in the initial project plan. Rather than ignore what they learned and build to the "contract," the Agile team can instead add customer reviews as an early feature. Although it may sound simple to just make the change, in reality there may be a big cost and impact on time. Agile helps expose these costs and time commitments, so the team (business, technology, and UX) can come to a shared understanding of the investment needed to deliver, and how it may be prioritized against other work. IAs with their research and design skills can have a big role in helping Agile teams pivot and learn about features, working with other stakeholders and users. The spirit of collaboration and including users is followed in all of the frameworks we discuss below.

> We are uncovering better ways of developing software by doing it and helping others do it.
> Through this work we have come to value:
>
> **Individuals and interactions** over processes and tools
> **Working software** over comprehensive documentation
> **Customer collaboration** over contract negotiation
> **Responding to change** over following a plan
>
> That is, while there is value in the items on the right, we value the items on the left more.

Figure 9.3: The Agile Manifesto (Beck et al., 2001).

9.2.2 DESIGN THINKING

Design Thinking is an approach to creating new ideas for solving problems from a user-centered perspective. Producing the final working code is not a part of design thinking; here we are trying to generate product ideas. Where the frameworks like Agile include development, design thinking is meant to take a deep dive into learning about users, their wants and needs, and developing ideas that solve problems. Organizations as varied as IBM, SAP, Uber, and GE use a design-thinking framework to iteratively develop new products and services. The goal is to provide solutions to user needs by learning about the problem space, and iterating through potential solutions, finding those that work (and those that don't work).

The steps in design thinking, (Figure 9.4) as developed by the Stanford "d.school" (Stanford University Institute of Design, 2016), include:

- **empathize:** understand users and their needs through user research;

- **define:** create a point of view, define the problem from a user perspective;

- **ideate:** think and develop a broad range of ideas to solve the problem;

- **prototype:** build a test system (even if it's a paper prototype) for users to interact with; and

- **test:** test the prototypes with users and iterate.

Figure 9.4: The design thinking process.

The process is shown in as a linear progression, but in practice it has many iterations and potential jumps backward. In fact, a big challenge in explaining iterative design is illustrating the many steps back. An online image search for design thinking shows an array of illustrations, from the (too) simple to the (unreadable) complex. In the real world, the team revisits previous work based on new learning and refines their ideas. Design thinking is a very popular topic for organizations large and small, leading to several "flavors" or unique takes on the methods, which can become confusing. We like the short and simple "bootcamp bootleg" published by Stanford at: https://dschool.stanford.edu/. In our experience it's proven to be the most concise and simple way to approach design thinking.

9.2.3   LEAN UX

Lean UX (Gothelf and Seiden, 2013) is based on three foundations: design thinking, Agile software development, and the lean startup method (Ries, 2011). Borrowing from these areas, the aim of Lean UX is to have collaborative teams constantly testing new features with users, and learning from their feedback. Eric Reis first proposed lean methodology as a way of developing new products and business ideas. Lean relies on learning from customers and users, rapidly validating ideas, and evolving products and solutions. Each idea is seen as a hypothesis to be tested, as quickly and efficiently as possible. IAs can adopt Lean principles (Lean UX) as a way to structure projects, gather user feedback, and guide the iterative design of information spaces.

The Lean UX process starts with declaring assumptions, developing a problem statement, and transforming assumptions into a hypothesis—how we think we can solve the problem. Hypotheses in Lean UX include creating personas and describing features and outcomes. Next, a Minimum Viable Product (MVP) is created, which is often a functioning prototype of a system or feature, and is analogous to conceptual designs in the processes we've described previously. Finally, the MVP is tested with users, and the feedback used to plan the next steps. Lean often uses a "canvas" to plan process and work; an example of a Lean UX Canvas is available from Jeff Gothelf's website: http://www.jeffgothelf.com/blog/leanuxcanvas/.

9.2.4   ROCKET SURGERY MADE EASY

Steve Krug, an influential usability researcher and author, suggests "a round of testing once a month, with three users" (Krug, 2010, p. 23). This method of small, regularly scheduled rounds of testing helps to identify usability issues that can be fixed in the next round of development. Krug's method can be adapted into existing design/development cycles, and he suggests modifying the number of participants if testing takes place more frequently. However, Krug cautions testing should not take place less than once a month, the point being that continuous feedback from users is necessary to find and fix usability problems.

Frameworks Summary

Agile, Lean, and other development frameworks like GV Design Sprints discussed earlier in Chapter 3 put an emphasis on user research in an iterative process. Nielsen (2007) concisely explains the need for research in the design and development frameworks described above: "How can designers find out what customers need? Through user research." We sometimes ask: "How do you know what users want? Ask them."

9.3   UX DECISION SUPPORT FRAMEWORK

While user research is essential for IA and user experience, IAs can also use their experience, theories, and secondary research to collect information and inform design.

Here, we present a decision support framework that brings together several pieces we've covered throughout the book, which was first shared at a UX workshop in 2015 (Zarro, 2015). Over the years as researchers and practitioners, we've seen projects where design by committee happens, or IA work is not implemented. A common thread of these projects is that when teams understand where the design concepts originate, risks are lowered (but never eliminated) and the chance of success increases.

Our framework has three main goals:

1. A process for making IA design decisions.

2. A way to reduce uncertainty in IA decision-making.

3. A way to support decisions in team discussions about IA research and design.

IAs should plan projects to include research, design, and evaluation as structured activities conducted in a user-centered process. Throughout the book we've covered these topics in depth. Sometimes in practice however, projects rely on a "fingers crossed" approach: The system will be usable even though design decisions are not supported by research. (In this case, witnessing the effects of users interacting with the final product is actually your research and evaluation process—far from ideal.) We may get lucky, "even a broken clock is right twice a day," but far more likely users will encounter avoidable issues, and the project's success will be less than its potential. Our framework provides a structured approach to making design decisions even when time and resources are severely limited.

IAs should support their decisions with data sources and findings. In our experience primary research is always a clear winner. There is just no substitute for meeting with users, "you always learn something new." However, in many cases other researchers have published relevant research or there is an HCI theory, pattern, or principle available to support design decision. It's likely that "someone has thought about your problem before and expressed those thoughts somehow" (Bernsen and Dybkjær, 2009), which you can use to augment primary research findings. Combining different methods (called triangulation) is very powerful and compelling. Think about the methods below like ingredients in a recipe. You can mix and match them to find what works best.

9.3.1   FIVE METHODS

1. **Thinking and Experience**

    a. What do we know as experienced IAs?

    b. What do we know we don't know, and how can we find out?

2. **Theory**

    a. What can we learn from HCI, IA, and related theories?

3. **Patterns and Principles**

    a. What can we reuse from the patterns and principles we see in similar contexts?

4. **Secondary Research**

    a. What can we learn from published academic research with empirical data?

    b. What can we learn from published case studies or projects lacking empirical data, outside of our organization?

    c. What can we learn from previous projects or research completed within our organization?

5. **Primary Research**

    a. What can we learn from our user research and evaluation efforts directly related to the current project?

Below, we explain the methods in more detail.

Thinking and Experience

Using thinking and experience, an IA can draw upon past projects and their capabilities to support their design decisions. If an IA has a lot of past experience applicable to a project, they can use that background to guide decision making. Bernsen classifies thinking as solving problems, and also identifying areas that it may not solve: "Thinking is as much an approach to discovering and solving problems as to deciding that certain problems *cannot* be solved through developer thinking alone but require other sources and methods to be resolved" (Bernsen and Dybkjær, 2009). IAs always use some level of thinking and experience in their designs, but need to be aware that many times this is not enough to produce optimal designs.

    Examples:

      "I've designed three dozen login forms, I know what this form needs"

      "This is a really complex problem, we'll need extensive research to understand how users will interact with the feature"

Theory

Theories offer a way to support decisions using academically supported ideas by sharing the "scientific foundations that underpin good design" (Bowles, 2010). We've listed several important HCI/IA theories and laws in an earlier chapter, and recommend going back to them during a design project to see how they may apply. Over time, it becomes second nature and you may feel like theories are almost collaborators, providing steady guidance. Although our example below may seem extreme it illustrates the powers of theory. Imagine designing software to be used in a medical setting or in an airplane cockpit.

    Example:

      "Hick's Law tells me that the more options I have, the longer it takes to make a decision. Let's not put any more links near the 'Abort self-destruction' button."

Patterns and Principles

We covered patterns and principles in Chapter 8. Across information spaces, UI elements and interaction become standard so it makes sense to follow convention. They are sometimes referred to as "best practices," and remember the saying, "recognition over recall." A design may follow others in an organization, may be similar to others in a domain (like libraries or financial websites), or may inherit general patterns from the web. Users likely have learned from other sites and apps they use. Several patterns and principles developed in web and mobile persist across many systems, providing a good head start for IA design. In particular, Microsoft, Apple, and Google have done a lot to standardize patterns on their hardware and in their software designs, because they control so much of our digital ecosystem. However, IAs should be aware of the "me too" designs. Don't rely on others too much or too often; it may mean you are not innovating or addressing the real needs of your users.

Example:

> "I need to design a mobile friendly, responsive website. Let's have the navigation roll-up into a hamburger menu on smartphones, we see that on a million sites."

Secondary Research

Secondary research is using the research published or shared by others to support your own work. Common sources for this include academic research and reports or whitepapers. Many academic researchers have published useful articles describing usability tests and other studies, which we can use to help design features. Just like in graduate school, we've had good success citing research papers in IA design deliverables even as practitioners.

You must develop critical evaluation skills when using other's research to inform your work, particularly for sources like blogs and others found online. In the graduate courses that form the basis of this book, we require that sources cited include some sort of data to back up their assertions—blogs and many web articles fall short here. Look into the context and reasoning behind articles—ensure they are relevant to your project and there is there evidence to support the conclusions.

Examples:

> "I need to design a faceted search tool for the college's academic libraries. I'll look at some academic research papers by information science professors."

> "We redesigned the college's website search 3 years ago, let's look through research deliverables from that project and see if there's anything relevant for our new project."

Primary Research

The gold standard for any project is conducting research and evaluation with the users of the system. Primary research puts the "focus on the user and not the product" (Barnum, 2010). In the previous methods there was no direct access to the user; they were not directly included in the design process. As we've learned, including users in the research process reduces the risk of building things that people do not want, or that do not work. In the medical field for example, it is not unheard of for doctors and nurses to refuse a system because poor usability hinders their ability to care. Quantitative measures and qualitative user quotes are extremely powerful when used to support design decisions.

Examples:

"I need to design a tool allowing users to self-register for their courses, let's talk to college students and find out how they register, and how we can improve the process."

"We just built a self-registration prototype, let's see how it performs with students."

9.3.2 USING THE FRAMEWORK

The UX decision support framework has three main uses. First, it can be used to structure information gathering activities, almost like a checklist of where to look for relevant facts or ideas when making design decisions. For example, conceptual designs could be roughly based on experience, theories, and patterns—and then evaluated with primary research. Or, in a resource-limited environment, when a critical piece of functionality is designed it should be based on primary research with theoretical support, while a minor part of the design could rely on less resource intensive principles and patterns.

Second, use the framework as a way to understand how and why design decisions were made. By recognizing the methods(s) used in the decision making process, teams can mitigate the risk of design decisions that are not supported by a strong foundation. While primary research should be most persuasive, the other methods can provide substantial objective data to support a design. For example, designs that are supported only by theory are not necessarily poor but may be made stronger through triangulation, reexamining them with one or more of the other methods.

Finally, it is almost inevitable that in a team environment differences of opinions will arise. Our framework is intended to support IAs in UX design "debates" (Bowles, 2010), and get to the best decision possible. People who work in the technology or business side of a project are unlikely to know the nuances of IA work, or the UX team members may have opposing viewpoints. Discussing the decision making process, along with the strengths and weaknesses of the methods used and some relevant data, goes a long way toward building confidence in the final decision. We sometimes compare this to "showing your work" on math problems in primary school or citing your sources in a college paper.

9.4   SUMMARY

IAs today are working on larger and larger projects that seem to become more and more complex. Across many industries and domains, a focus on the value of user experiences is increasing. In order to improve efficiency and be more user-focused, design and development teams are structured in ways that bring together various disciplines and help them work toward a common goal, but there is no one-size-fits-all approach. Although IAs are highly involved in just some parts of a project, their work is instrumental throughout the entire process. UX team members may be generalists, with expertise across domains or specialists who focus on one area. Those who can combine generalist and specialist traits (T-shaped) can be quite valuable to a team.

Overall, the information technology industry has taken steps toward user-centered approaches that incorporate user feedback, closely aligning with IA and UX concepts. We presented a decision support framework which incorporates several of the concepts in our previous chapters, and should help IAs structure information-gathering activities and share the decision-making process with others.

CHAPTER   10

The Future of IA

"The future is already here — it's just not very evenly distributed" —attributed to the author William Gibson

Over the past nine chapters we have discussed the history of IA, research methods and tools, design and design implications, and IA applications in enterprises, web, mobile, and in the global setting. Coming to this closing chapter, let's take one more look at IA itself, with a particular curiosity of its future in mind. What brings the IA community together and where will it lead us? What are the future trends in IA design? What are the relationships between IA practice and IA research? How can IAs structure make the maximum impact in organizations? In this chapter, we will discuss these questions and look beyond horizons for the future of information architecture.

10.1   GLOBAL IA

As the internet brings people around the world closer and closer together, IAs will have more opportunities to create systems for a global audience, especially on the "world wide" web. Particularly in developing regions, IA priorities may be different due to a reliance on mobile devices or other factors (some areas went from no internet directly to mobile only, bypassing much of web1.0 and web2.0). While global information architecture covers a lot of topics, in this section we focus on the user experience strategy for institutions that need to interact with their users in multiple languages/cultures, from different countries, or in a combination of both. People from different cultures and countries have different value systems and cognitive styles, which may lead to different expectations and interpretations of their Web user experience and usability. Companies and businesses with global distributions of services and products need to pay close attention to those factors so that they can design their user interfaces accordingly to best meet the user needs.

10.1.1   MAKEUP OF THE WORLD'S INTERNET USERS

The internet was invented in the Western, English-speaking world. However, as globalization accelerates, the percentage of non-Western, non-English-speaking (as a first language) users has been growing rapidly (Table 10.1). Today there are an estimated 3.2 billion internet users, and you may be surprised at the finding, "for every Internet user in the developed world there are 2 in the developing world" (ICT Data and Statistics Division, 2015). The percentage of internet users ranges from 98.3% of the population in Bermuda, to just 1.1% in Eritrea (The World Bank, 2015). And in every region but Africa more than half of the population use the internet or use a smartphone (Pew Research Center, 2016).

Table 10.1: Number of internet users by language (Internet World Stats, 2016) http://www.internetworldstats.com/stats7.htm

Language	# of users	% Total Internet Users	Growth (2000–2016)
English	948,608,782	67.8 %	573.9 %
Chinese	751,985,224	53.1 %	2,227.9 %
Spanish	277,125,947	61.6 %	1,424.3 %
Arabic	168,426,690	43.4 %	6,602.5 %
Portuguese	154,525,606	57.9 %	1,939.7 %
Japanese	115,111,595	91.0 %	144.5 %
Malay	109,400,982	37.8 %	1,809.3 %
Russian	103,147,691	70.5 %	3,227.3 %
French	102,171,481	25.9 %	751.5 %
German	83,825,134	88.3 %	204.6 %
Other Languages	797,046,681	22.1 %	1,141.0 %
Total	3,611,375,813	100 %	900.4 %

10.1.2   THE NEED FOR INTERNATIONALIZATION AND LOCALIZATION

Globalization makes it possible for companies to gain significantly bigger portions of sales outside of their domestic markets. Nike sells its products in over 100 countries, and McDonalds is also operating in over 100 countries. It is key to success for those multinational companies to understand the local markets, and position products and services appropriately. Also, it is equally important to understand and meet the needs of employees in different regions and countries to boost collaboration and improve job productivity.

All of this points to IAs focusing on internationalization and localization for websites, apps, and intranets. While *internationalization* (I18N) is about designing an application or website so that it can be adapted to various languages and regions without engineering changes, *localization* is the process of adapting the website through language, content, and design to reflect local cultural sensitivities. In short, multinational/multilingual websites should be functionally intuitive and culturally appropriate for all intended audiences.

A lot of subtle or significant differences need to be taken into consideration in cultural preferences, language, tradition, religion, etc. The next section introduces how cross-cultural theories help guide the localization of website designs.

10.1.3   CROSS-CULTURE THEORIES AND LOCALIZATION

Here, we introduce two sets of well-known cross-culture theories that can be used to guide the user experience strategies for localization. One is Edward Hall's theory about High-Context (HC) vs. Low-Context (LC) cultures (1989), and the other is Hofstede's Cultural Dimensions framework (1984). In addition, empirical studies also show evidence that people from different cultures interpret usability differently. Even the way they organize information is different (Frandsen-Thorlacius et al., 2009; Morville, 2003).

High-context vs. Low-context Culture Types

Hall states that all cultures can be situated in relation to one another through the styles in which they communicate. In low-context cultures, such as France, North America, Scandinavian countries, and German-speaking countries, low-context communication occurs predominantly through *explicit* statements in text and speech—the mass of the information is vested in the explicit code. As such, most of the information must be in the transmitted message in order to make up for what is missing in the context. High-context cultures, including Japan, Arab countries, Greece, Spain, Italy, and England, involve *implying* a message through that which is not spoken; messages include other communication cues such as body language, eye movement, para-verbal cues, and the use of silence. HC communication is identified as indirect, ambiguous, maintaining of harmony, reserved and understated. In contrast, LC communication is identified as direct, precise, dramatic, open, and based on feelings or true intentions.

The HC and LC theory has been applied to guide international website design. By studying McDonalds' country-specific websites, Würtz (2005) found a set of differences among local websites of the same company.

- Websites in HC tend to use more animated effects than those in LC.

- Low-context websites are expected to be consistent in their layout and color schemes, whereas pages in high-context websites are expected to be diverse.

- Opening of links in the same browser windows in LC websites is in contrast to the HC Asian websites where new pages would open in new browser windows, giving the visitor a multitude of starting points for further website navigation.

Hofstede's Five Cultural Dimensions

Overview of the Five Dimensions

Based on his five years of intensive research with hundreds of IBM employees in 53 countries, Dutch cultural anthropologist Geert Hofstede identified five cultural dimensions. He rated all the 53 countries on indices for each dimension, normalized to values (usually) of 0–100. The five dimensions of culture are as follows:

- **Power-distance:** the extent to which the less powerful members of institutions and organizations within a country expect and accept that power is distributed unequally.

- **Collectivism vs. individualism:** individualism pertains to societies in which the ties between individuals are loose; everyone is expected to look after himself or herself and his/her immediate family. Collectivism pertains to societies in which people from birth onward are integrated into strong, cohesive in-groups, which throughout people's lifetime continue to protect them in exchange for unquestioning loyalty.

- **Femininity vs. masculinity:** masculinity pertains to societies in which social gender roles are clearly distinct; femininity pertains to societies in which social gender roles overlap.

- **Uncertainty avoidance (UA):** the extent to which people feel anxiety about uncertain or unknown matters. Cultures with high UA tend to have more formal rules, and focus on tactical operations rather than strategy. People seem active, emotional, and even aggressive. By contrast, low UA cultures tend to be more informal and focus more on long-range strategic matters than day-to-day operations. These cultures tend to be less expressive and less openly anxious; people behave quietly without showing aggression or strong emotions; people seem easy-going and relaxed.

- **Long vs. short-term orientation:** long-term dimension is also called "Confucian dynamism." Persistence (perseverance), ordering relationships by status and observing this order, thrift and having a sense of shame are the dominant values. The values of perseverance and thrift are future oriented and more dynamic, while the short-term values are more static, being past and present oriented.

Implications of Cultural Dimensions on Design

When using cultural dimensions as a framework to analyze websites, researchers (Frandsen-Thorlacius et al., 2009; Marcus and Gould, 2000) reported the following distinctive user experience focuses from different cultures. LC cultures tend to have low scores in Power Distance and Uncertainty Avoidance, and more Collectivism oriented; and vice versa. Both LC/HC theory and the Uncertainty Avoidance dimension can well explain why Europeans expect compact web pages with a few precise links, while many Asian consumers on high-bandwidth networks expect results as screens full of colorful content.

Guidelines for Global IA and User Experience Design

There are two common ways to localize information systems:

- a surface-level translation of language and jargon to reflect the conventions of the target audience; and

- a deeper aesthetic change, altering images, colors, logic, functionality, and branding to conform to the target audience on a cultural level (Sun, 2001).

Below are some specific guidelines for globalization.

- **Pay Attention to Language Details:** Translation is by no means straightforward. Sometimes, there is no direct mapping between languages, and people in different cultures interpret words/meanings differently. For example, the word "flat" in Nebraska is not the same as a "flat" in London.

- **Text Swell:** The difference between the width of text between various languages. Typically, German translations require 30%–40% more space than English. Sometimes, while some English labels or phrases can fit in one line, in German it would require text wrapping. Be aware of left-to-right and right-to-left translations.

- **The Combination of Languages and Countries:** Most countries speak multiple languages and some languages are spoken in multiple countries. Do not assume that there is one-to-one mapping between each country/region and the official language of the country.

- **Language options need to be obvious and easy to find:** Otherwise, most people would assume there are no such options. List choices in the target language, not English.

- **Avoid Using Non-Universal Symbols and Iconographies:** Be sensitive to the customs and practices of other cultures. For example, the "okay" sign (index finger and thumb together forming a circle) is considered obscene in Brazil, while the thumbs-up gesture in Iran is highly offensive.

- **Colors Have Cultural Significance:** It is imperative that you do your homework before you choose colors for your international website (Iler, 2007). For example, black in Western culture is the color of mourning; not so in Asia, where white signifies death.

- **Understanding Cultural Subtlety:** In the Chinese culture, almost all names have some meaning, especially for company names or trademarks. Company names are often considered as the equivalent of their brands.

- **Beware of Users' Environmental Situations:** For example, multiple family members may share one account in collectivism cultures (e.g., in Vietnam). People may sit side by side to browse the web together. Under these circumstances, system features like shared accounts and co-browsing should be taken into consideration.

- **Supporting Global eCommerce:** In North America, the standard purchase method has been credit cards. However, that is not the case in some European or Asian countries. In Germany, many people prefer to pay by cash or money order, and in China credit cards are not as widespread as in the U.S.

Global IA Summary

Global IA is growing in importance as more people around the world, particularly in developing regions, access the internet. Western/English speaking is the predominate paradigm for many today, but IAs should be aware that their work can reach a worldwide audience. Designing for a global product is challenging, however with new web-based technologies, user research and design efforts can be coordinated around the globe from a central location, connecting IAs with a new global audience.

10.2   THE FUTURE OF IA

Let's take one more look at IA itself, with a particular curiosity of its future in mind. What brings the IA community together? What are the trends in IA design? What are the relationships between IA practice and IA research? Let's discuss these questions and look to the future of information architecture.

10.2.1   THE IA COMMUNITY

In the last edition of this book, we asked: Will IA be established as a new field, a new profession, or a new way of thinking? We think the answer to this all three is "yes," with some qualifications. IA has been established as a field, within the domain of user experience. IA is also a profession, but is sometimes lumped together with UX designer and related disciplines, without distinguishing the nuances. Because one person often plays more than just the IA role on a team, differentiating professions can be a challenge. IAs are in demand, and have substantial impact on information organizations. Organizing information and looking across devices and channels is a growing area. Finally, as a new way of thinking? Yes—the structure and integration of information spaces, and the connections between them is undoubtedly a huge topic today. In fact, with so many design patterns and principles, architecting and connecting different components can be the bulk of an IA's work.

However, IA does still seem to lack an academic research "home base." IA does not appear to be a standalone discipline—but we are not sure that it matters. University IA courses are taught in many programs like library and information science, although departments of Information Architecture have not taken hold. We think in some ways this speaks to the appeal of IA, that its inter-disciplinary nature means it can be taught and researched as part of other academic disciplines.

Despite its short history and lack of an academic research home base, the IA community is steadily growing. One of the premier gathering places for the IA community is the IA Summit conference held each year since 2000 (http://iasummit.org/). Information architects, user experience professionals, researchers, and thinkers gather together to share their experience and define the emerging field. Below we show a list of IA Summit themes since its inception.

- 2000: Defining Information Architecture

- 2001: Practicing Information Architecture

- 2002: Refining our Craft

- 2003: Making Connections

- 2004: Breaking New Ground

- 2005: Crossing

- 2006: Learning, Doing, Selling

- 2007: Enriching IA

- 2008: Experiencing Information

- 2009: Expanding our Horizons

- 2010: This One Goes to Eleven

- 2011: Asking Better Questions

- 2012: Cross Your Channels

- 2013: Observe, Build, Share, Repeat

- 2014: The Path Ahead

- 2015: Reclaiming Information Architecture

- 2016: A Broader Panorama

- 2017: Designing for Humans. IA, meet AI

The trend in the list is clear: IA has moved from defining itself, to defining its practices and knowledge base, to enriching and expanding IA as a discipline, and on to integrating with other disciplines like artificial intelligence.

In addition to the Summit and other events, the IA community is supported by a number of resources. Below is a brief list of major IA related organizations and resources.

NN/g: Nielsen Norman Group

https://www.nngroup.com

> This is an absolute thought leader in the field of HCI, usability, user experience design, and information architecture. We've cited this source throughout our book: "NN/g conducts groundbreaking research, evaluates user interfaces, and reports real findings—not just what's popular or expected."

UIE: User Interface Engineering

https://articles.uie.com/

> Another good resource for research articles that illustrate key IA points and provides great examples: "User Interface Engineering is a leading research, training, and consulting firm specializing in website and product usability."

MeasuringU

http://www.measuringu.com/blog.php

> A good place for examples on the quantitative side of IA and UX, provides many excellent insights into standardized questionnaires and usability measures: "MeasuringU provides more than intuition and qualitative insights about products and designs. We provide meaning through measurement."

ASIS&T: The Association for Information Science and Technology

https://www.asist.org

> ASIS&T is the organization that hosts the IA summit and supports information professionals and organizations.

ACM: The Association for Computing Machinery

http://www.acm.org

ACM is "the world's largest educational and scientific computing society." In particular, IAs would be most interested in the special interest group SIGCHI (http://www.acm.org/special-interest-groups/sigs/sigchi), and the ACM digital library.

Information Architecture Institute

http://www.iainstitute.org

Seeming to be undergoing reorganization, the IA institute may yet prove to be a valuable central hub for IA.

Boxes and Arrows

http://boxesandarrows.com

Boxes and Arrows provides articles and discussions written by leading experts, in the fields of "graphic design, interaction design, information architecture and the design of business."

IxDA: The Interaction Design Association

http://ixda.org

IxDA supports professionals in the Interaction Design community, with a goal of advancing the human condition through better design.

InfoDesign

http://www.informationdesign.org

Provides links to articles and blog posts of interest to IAs and related disciplines.

Community Events

In addition to the IA summit, the IA community also has two other major community-run, in-person events:

- European IA Summit, which is held every year in Europe: http://www.euroia.org

- World IA Day, a one-day celebration of IA with events around the world: http://worldiaday.org

10.3 NEW CHALLENGES FOR INFORMATION ARCHITECTS

The information technology environment has constantly changed over the last two decades. While information architecture emerged from a need to create more usable websites, information architects are no longer just website designers. They are also information designers, interaction designers, navigation designers, usability designers, user experience designers, content strategists, and information strategy designers, just to name a few. This expansion of the role of information architects brings new opportunities as well as new responsibilities and challenges that come with the opportunities. In the following, we briefly discuss some of the new challenges.

10.3.1 FINDABILIITY AND CROSS-CHANNEL/UBIQUITOUS ACCESS

Findability has long been established as an essential task for IA (Morville, 2005). Today findability and refindabilty across channels and devices is a key area for IA. As people move to a multi-device experience, some information may be useful in multiple contexts. Would it be possible, for example, for a smartphone to detect the TV show a user is watching and automatically search for updates on social media?

Content created on one device is likely to be needed on another, leading IAs to investigate cross-channel experiences. As we discussed in Chapter 1: Accessing, consuming, and creating information is increasingly decoupled from the device and more tied to the individual user, who often has access to several devices. The cloud in particular serves as a technological foundation for these experiences. The forward-looking IA will learn about these technologies and how to leverage them for new and innovative user experiences. People want access to information anytime, anywhere.

10.3.2 CONTENT REPRESENTATION

Content representation traditionally focuses on designing content organization systems based on semantic relationships of terms and concepts. As if this is not hard enough, for information architecture, content representation is hardly single-dimensional, based on semantics only. Social networks, linked data that come from different sources, and content semantics are often intertwined to challenge the design skills of information architects. Many unsolved problems related to content representation, such as automatic metadata generation, controlled vocabularies and user's tagging integration, and using semantic networks for access and navigation, are very difficult challenges both for research and for implementations.

10.3.3 DIGITAL PRESERVATION

What happens to all this new information being created and stored (and that can be deleted without a trace)? How can we track changes to dynamic, database-backed websites (assuming we should)? How can users maintain different versions of documents on their device and cloud? Should information architects be responsible for these challenges? The answer is it depends on the preservation need, but IAs should certainly have an influence on any preservation efforts .

In the physical space, things are expected to last. If a building collapses 100 years after it is built, people will trace back to the original architects to check if the collapse was due to a faulty design. In the digital space, things are much more dynamic. As information comes and goes, people may not have access to the digital content available a few years ago. And as more companies rely on the digital space for their business, preserving content and data over a longer period of time has become important. Some businesses even have what are called "data warehouses" that store all sorts of data and content. Digital preservation techniques are needed to maintain access, and in some cases to comply with legal or other regulations. IAs can support preservation through metadata and design.

10.3.4 VOICE AND GESTURE

Voice interfaces like Apple's SIRI and Amazon Echo are becoming mainstream. They can be used to perform basic lookups and commands, with new features constantly developed. A new paradigm is the always-on microphone, simply by saying "Hey Alexa" a user can begin interaction with Amazon's Alexa service through their echo device. This book and other information architecture texts tend to avoid discussion of voice and gesture, as it is still considered a specialized topic area—although that is likely to change in the coming years.

Gesture input is characterized usually by a touch screen, where swipes and multi-finger actions perform different tasks. IAs must be aware of limitations like the lack of onHover in a touch environment. Other devices like Microsoft's Kinect motion-sensing input and Tobii's eye-tracking input are offering more and more features that use eye or body movement for commands. As these technologies develop we can expect to see them leveraged in new and innovative ways.

Additionally, IAs should look at the technologies built into smartphones as new types of "user input," including movement and biometric sensors.

10.3.5 CUSTOMER EXPERIENCE

Customer experience is a field that follows a customer (user) across all the "touchpoints" in relation to an organization. Touchpoints can include things like websites, in-person/in-store, and calling a customer care line. An important concept is that of the "customer journey," which shows interactions along with motivations, emotions, and outcomes. Increasingly the work of IAs is included as part of a customer experience program, and as experts in understanding users—IAs are sensible choices to help lead these efforts. Personalization, customization, and the context of use seem to be growing in importance as the "one-size-fits-all" approach is being left behind.

10.4   IA AND RESEARCH

IA is defined by some as both art and science. As art, IA needs to be learned through practice. There are a growing number of IA books, conferences, blogs, and various publications that focus on IA practice, and related disciplines like user experience and usability research. Through sharing design experience, case studies, and lessons learned, the IA community enriches the IA process, methodology, and skill sets.

The science part of IA appears to be less developed in a traditional sense. IA in general depends on related domains' theories and methods to guide its development, although there have been calls for dedicated research in the IA community. Information Architecture books and reports have been published that further the field, even if not in always in an "academic" setting.

It may be that Information Architecture is an emerging type of research domain—one in which basic research is in fact applied research (Zarro and Carvin, 2011), where there is a "reverse flow, from technology to science," and where "more and more science has become *technology* derived" (Stokes, 1997). Perhaps the science of IA is really the integration of diverse research and data streams to further the design of information spaces.

We believe that it is important to continue conducting IA-related research, under any domain's name. The IA community will help document "what works and what does not work" when we adopt knowledge from other fields to IA. It will also help to understand design issues and prevent "re-inventing the wheel" when IA practitioners face similar problems again and again. More importantly, the field of IA needs new ideas that can only be established through rigorous research and through the dialogs between researchers and practitioners.

10.5   IA AND BEYOND

Before we end this journey in the land of information architecture, let us revisit our description of information architects given in Chapter 1:

> Information architecture is about organizing and simplifying information for its intended users; designing, integrating, and aggregating information spaces to create usable systems or interfaces; creating ways for people to find, understand, exchange and manage information; and, therefore, stay on top of information and make the right decisions.

We hope that it becomes clearer now that the point we emphasize throughout the book is that IA is not just about UI design or backend metadata and content. Rather, IA is about helping people make use of information and make information spaces work for them. Like building architects who deal with *site*, *space*, and *place* and whose goal is to convert a site into a place where space can be experienced, information architects' ultimate mission is to integrate information spaces into places where users can have productive and fulfilling experiences, and where information is fully utilized to support people's goals and extend their abilities.

Bibliography

Abramson, N. (1970). The aloha system: Another alternative for computer communications. In *Proceedings of the November 17-19, 1970, Fall Joint Computer Conference* (pp. 281–285). ACM:New York, NY, USA. DOI: 10.1145/1478462.1478502. 12

Alexander, C. (1979). *The Timeless Way of Building* (Vol. 1). Oxford University Press:New York. 99

American Academy of Orthopaedic Surgeons. (2015). Distracted walking study: Topline summary findings. American Academy of Orthopaedic Surgeons. Retrieved from http://www.anationinmotion.org/wp-content/uploads/2015/12/AAOS-Distracted-Walking-Topline-11-30-15.pdf. 107

Apple. (2016). UI Design Do's and Don'ts - Apple Developer. Retrieved December 17, 2016, from https://developer.apple.com/design/tips/. 105

Apple Computer Inc. (1993). *Macintosh Human Interface Guidelines* (2nd edition). Addison-Wesley Professional: Reading, MA. 100

Barnum, C. M. (2010). *Usability Testing Essentials: Ready, Set... Test!* Elsevier. 126

Bates, M. J. (1989). The design of browsing and berrypicking techniques for the online search interface. *Online Information Review*, 13(5), 407–424. DOI: 10.1108/eb024320. 80

Beck, K., Beedle, M., Bennekum, A. van, Cockburn, A., Cunningham, W., Fowler, M., Grenning, J., Highsmith, J., Hunt, A., Jeffries, R., Kern, J., Marick, B., Martin, R. C., Mellor, S., Schwaber, K., Sutherland, J., and Thomas, D. (2001). Manifesto for Agile Software Development. Retrieved December 18, 2016, from http://agilemanifesto.org/. 119, 120

Belkin, N. J., Oddy, R. N., and Brooks, H. M. (1982). ASK for information retrieval: Part I. Background and theory. *Journal of Documentation*, 38(2), 61–71. DOI: 10.1108/eb026722. 73

Benedek, J. and Miner, T. (2002). Measuring desirability: New methods for evaluating desirability in a usability lab setting. *Proceedings of Usability Professionals Association*, 2003, 8–12.

Bernsen, N. O. and Dybkjær, L. (2009). *Multimodal Usability*. Human-Computer Interaction Series. Springer-Verlag:London, 1. DOI: 10.1007/978-1-84882-553-6. 123, 124

Beyer, H. and Holtzblatt, K. (1997). *Contextual Design: A Customer-Centered Approach to Systems Designs*. Morgan Kaufmann Series in Interactive Technologies. Morgan Kaufmann. 25

Blandford, A., Furniss, D., and Makri, S. (2016). Qualitative HCI Research: Going Behind the Scenes. *Synthesis Lectures on Human-Centered Informatics*, Morgan & Claypool Publishers. 9(1), 1–115. DOI: 10.2200/S00706ED1V01Y201602HCI034. 47

Bowles, C. (2010). *Winning a User Experience Debate*. Retrieved December 28, 2016, from http://www.uxbooth.com/articles/winning-a-user-experience-debate/. 124, 126

Brooke, J. (2013). SUS: A Retrospective. *JUS. Journal of Usability Studies*, 8(2), 29–40. 55

Budiu, R. (2016). The power law of learning: Consistency vs. innovation in user interfaces. Retrieved December 17, 2016, from https://www.nngroup.com/articles/power-law-learning/. 100

Bush, V. (1945, July). As We May Think. *The Atlantic*. Retrieved from http://www.theatlantic.com.ezproxy2.library.drexel.edu/magazine/archive/1945/07/as-we-may-think/3881/?single_page=true. 12

Buxton, W. and Sniderman, R. (1980). Iteration in the design of the human-computer interface. In *Proceedings of the 13th Annual Meeting of the Human Factors Association of Canada* (Vol. 7281). 37

Card, S. K., Pirolli, P., Van Der Wege, M., Morrison, J. B., Reeder, R. W., Schraedley, P. K., and Boshart, J. (2001). Information scent as a driver of Web behavior graphs: results of a protocol analysis method for Web usability. In *Proceedings of the SIGCHI conference on Human Factors in Computing Systems* (pp. 498–505). ACM. DOI: 10.1145/365024.365331. 77

Chaiken, S. (1980). Heuristic versus systematic information processing and the use of source versus message cues in persuasion. *Journal of Personality and Social Psychology*, 39(5), 752. DOI: 10.1037/0022-3514.39.5.752. 78

Chevrolet. (n.d.). 4G LTE In-Car Wi-Fi: Features and Information | Chevrolet. Retrieved December 21, 2016, from http://www.chevrolet.com/4g-lte-in-car-wifi.html. 19

Cooper, A. (2004). *The Inmates Are Running the Asylum: Why High-tech Products Drive Us Crazy and How to Restore the Sanity*. Sams. 26, 49, 88

Diamond, F. (2003). Web traffic analytics and user experience. Retrieved December 24, 2016, from http://boxesandarrows.com/web-traffic-analytics-and-user-experience/. 52, 53

DiMicco, J. M., Millen, D. R., Geyer, W., Dugan, C., and Street, O. R. (2008). Research on the use of social software in the workplace. In *Conference Proceedings* (pp. 8–12). Citeseer. 18

Ding, W. (2009). Marriott IA Team Mission Statement. Internal Presentation. 117

Duyne, D. K. V., Landay, J., and Hong, J. I. (2002). *The Design of Sites: Patterns, Principles, and Processes for Crafting a Customer-centered Web Experience*. Addison-Wesley. 25

Executive Secretariat of the World Summit on the Information Society. (2005). *World Summit on the Information Society*. Retrieved December 10, 2016, from https://www.itu.int/net/wsis/basic/faqs.asp. 10

Fox, C. (2003). Sitemaps and site indexes: What they are and why you should have them. Boxes and Arrows. Retrieved December 22, 2016, from http://boxesandarrows.com/sitemaps-and-site-indexes-what-they-are-and-why-you-should-have-them/. 71

Frandsen-Thorlacius, O., Hornbæk, K., Hertzum, M., and Clemmensen, T. (2009). Non-universal usability?: a survey of how usability is understood by Chinese and Danish users. In *Proceedings of the SIGCHI Conference on Human Factors in Computing Systems* (pp. 41–50). ACM. DOI: 10.1145/1518701.1518708. 131, 132

Fraternali, P., Rossi, G., and Sánchez-Figueroa, F. (2010). Rich internet applications. *IEEE Internet Computing*, 14(3), 9–12. DOI: 10.1109/MIC.2010.76. 16

Frost, B. (2016). *Atomic Design*. Retrieved December 26, 2016, from http://atomicdesign.bradfrost.com/. 105

Garrett, J. (2002). *The Elements of User Experience: User-Centered Design for the Web*. Peachpit Press. 4

Garrett, J. J. (2005). *Ajax: A New Approach to Web Applications*. Retrieved December 27, 2016, from http://adaptivepath.org/ideas/ajax-new-approach-web-applications/. 96

George, A. (2014). *That Disastrous Car Homer Simpson Designed Was Actually Ahead of Its Time*. Retrieved December 12, 2016, from https://www.wired.com/2014/07/homer-simpson-car/.

Gerchev, I. (2012). *Build Your Perfect Interface with UI Design Patterns*. Retrieved December 17, 2016, from https://www.sitepoint.com/build-your-perfect-interface-with-ui-design-patterns/. 99

Gertner, J. (2012). *The Idea Factory*. London: Penguin. 12

Gilliland-Swetland, A., Bacca, M., and Gill, T. (2000). *Introduction to Metadata: Pathways to Digital Information*. Getty Information Institute. 60

Golder, S. A. and Huberman, B. A. (2006). Usage patterns of collaborative tagging systems. *Journal of Information Science*, 32(2), 198–208. DOI: 10.1177/0165551506062337. 16, 68

Google. (2015). *Second-Screen Searches: Crucial I-Want-to-Know Moments for Brands*. Retrieved December 11, 2016, from https://www.thinkwithgoogle.com/articles/second-screen-searches-crucial-i-want-to-know-moments-for-brands.html. 108

Google. (n.d.-a). *Accessibility - Usability - Material Design Guidelines*. Retrieved December 17, 2016, from https://material.io/guidelines/usability/accessibility.html#accessibility-principles. 106

Google. (n.d.-b). Introduction - Material design - Material design guidelines. Retrieved December 17, 2016, from https://material.io/guidelines/#introduction-principles. 106

Gothelf, J. and Seiden, J. (2013). *Lean UX: Applying Lean Principles to Improve User Experience.* O'Reilly Media, Inc. 121

Guenther, M. (2013). *Intersection: How Enterprise Design Bridges the Gap between Business, Technology, and People.* Morgan Kaufmann :Waltham, MA. 9

Guy, M. and Tonkin, E. (2006). Folksonomies: Tidying up tags? *D-Lib Magazine*, 12(1). Retrieved from http://www.dlib.org/dlib/january06/guy/01guy.html. DOI: 10.1045/january2006-guy. 66

Hafner, K. and Lyon, M. (1998). *Where Wizards Stay Up Late: The Origins of the Internet.* Simon and Schuster. 12

Hall, E. T. and Hall, M. R. (1989). *Understanding Cultural Differences.* Intercultural Press. 131

Hanson, N. (2013). Humanizing business technology. Design. Retrieved from http://www.slideshare.net/ndhanthro/humanizing-business-technology. 41

Hearst, M. (2009). *Search User Interfaces.* University Press:Cambridge. DOI: 10.1017/CBO9781139644082. 32, 73, 84

Hick, W. E. (1952). On the rate of gain of information. *Quarterly Journal of Experimental Psychology*, 4(1), 11–26. DOI: 10.1080/17470215208416600. 77

Hofstede, G. (1984). *Culture's Consequences: International Differences in Work-related Values.* Sage.

Hyman, R. (1953). Stimulus information as a determinant of reaction time. *Journal of Experimental Psychology*, 45(3), 188. DOI: 10.1037/h0056940. 77

ICT Data and Statistics Division. (2015). ICT Facts Figures 2015. Geneva, Switzerland: International Telecommunication Union. Retrieved from https://www.itu.int/en/ITU-D/Statistics/Documents/facts/ICTFactsFigures2015.pdf. 9, 129

Iler, H. (2007). It's in the details: Seven Secrets of a Successful International Website. Retrieved December 18, 2016, from http://www.digital-web.com/articles/secrets_of_a_successful_international_website/. 134

Internet World Stats. (2016). Top ten internet languages - World internet statistics. Retrieved December 18, 2016, from http://www.internetworldstats.com/stats7.htm. 130

ISO. (1998). ISO 9241-11:1998 Ergonomic requirements for office work with visual display terminals (VDTs) -- Part 11: Guidance on usability- Part 11: Guidance on usability. International Standardization Organization (ISO). Switzerland. Retrieved from http://www.iso.org/iso/catalogue_detail.htm?csnumber=16883. 30

ISO. (2010). ISO 9241-210: 2010. Ergonomics of human system interaction-Part 210: Human-centred design for interactive systems. International Standardization Organization (ISO). Switzerland. 39

IxDA. Interaction Design Association. (2009). *About Interaction Design*. Retrieved from http://www.ixda.org/about_interaction.php. 87

Jacobson, R. (ed.) (2000). *Information Design*. The MIT Press. 6

Kahn, P. and Lenk, K. (2001). *Mapping Websites*. Crans-Près-Céligny, Switzerland: RotoVision SA. 71

Kalfatovic, M. R., Kapsalis, E., Spiess, K. P., Van Camp, A., and Edson, M. (2009). Smithsonian team Flickr: A library, archives, and museums collaboration in web 2.0 space. *Archival Science*, 8(4), 267–277. DOI: 10.1007/s10502-009-9089-y. 66

Kelly, D. (2009). Methods for evaluating interactive information retrieval systems with users. *Foundations and Trends in Information Retrieval*, 3(1–2), 1–224. DOI: 10.1561/1500000012.

Kipfer, B. A. (1997). *The Order of Things: How Everything in the World Is Organized... Into Hierarchies, Structures, and Pecking Orders*. Random House. 57

Krug, S. (2005). *Don't Make Me Think: A Commonsense Approach to Web Usability* (2nd ed.). New Riders Press. 83

Krug, S. (2010). *Rocket Surgery Made Easy: The Do-it-yourself Guide to Finding and Fixing Usability Problems*. Berkeley, CA: New Riders. 122

Lakoff, G. (2008). *Women, Fire, and Dangerous Things: What Categories Reveal about the Mind*. Univ. of Chicago Press. Retrieved from http://books.google.com/books?id=TomacQAACAAJ. 80

Lidwell, W., Holden, K., and Butler, J. (2003). *Universal Principles of Design*. Rockport Pub. 77, 103

Madden, A. D., Eaglestone, B., Ford, N. J., and Whittle, M. (2007). Search engines: a first step to finding information: preliminary findings froma study of observed searches. Information Research, 12(2), paper 294. 84

Maes, P. (1994). Agents that reduce work and information overload. *Communications of the ACM*, 37(7), 30–40. DOI: 10.1145/176789.176792. 20

Marchionini, G. (2006). Exploratory Search: From finding to understanding. *Communications of the ACM*, 49(4), 41–46. DOI: 10.1145/1121949.1121979. 80

Marcotte, E. (2011). *Responsive Web Design*. A Book Apart. 10

Marcus, A. and Gould, E. (2000). Crosscurrents: cultural dimensions and global Web user-interface design. In *Proceedings 6th Conference on Human Factors and the Web*. DOI: 10.1145/345190.345238. 132

Marlow, C., Naaman, M., Boyd, D., and Davis, M. (2006). HT06, tagging paper, taxonomy, Flickr, academic article, to read. In *Proceedings of the Seventeenth Conference on Hypertext and Hypermedia* (pp. 31–40). ACM:New York. DOI: 10.1145/1149941.1149949. 16, 66

Mauer, D. (2006). Women, Fire, and Dangerous Things: What Every IA Should Know. In *IA Summit 2006 Lecture Notes*. 80

Merrill, D. (2006). *Mashups: The New Breed of Web App*. IBM Web Architecture Technical Library, 1–13. 13

Microsoft. (n.d.-a). *Following User Interface Guidelines*. Retrieved December 17, 2016, from https://msdn.microsoft.com/en-us/library/windows/desktop/ff728821(v=vs.85).aspx. 100

Microsoft. (n.d.-b). *How to Design a Great User Experience for Desktop Applications* (Windows). Retrieved December 17, 2016, from https://msdn.microsoft.com/library/windows/desktop/dn742462.aspx. 106

Miller, G. A. (1956). The magical number seven, plus or minus two: Some limits on our capacity for processing information. *Psychological Review*, 63(2), 81. DOI: 10.1037/h0043158. 76

Morville, P. (2003, July 14). *International Information Architecture*. Retrieved December 18, 2016, from http://semanticstudios.com/international_information_architecture/. 131

Morville, P. (2005). *Ambient Findability: What We Find Changes Who We Become*. O'Reilly Media. 74, 138

Morville, P. and Callender, J. (2010). *Search Patterns: Design for Discovery*. O'Reilly Media, Inc. 74

Morville, P., Rosenfield, L., and Arango, J. (2015). *Information Architecture for the Web and Beyond*, 4th Edition. 5

Müller, H., Gove, J. L., Webb, J. S., and Cheang, A. (2015). Understanding and Comparing Smartphone and Tablet Use: Insights from a Large-Scale Diary Study. In *Proceedings of the Annual Meeting of the Australian Special Interest Group for Computer Human Interaction* (pp. 427–436). ACM. DOI: 10.1145/2838739.2838748. 108

Myers, B. A. (1998). A brief history of human-computer interaction technology. *Interactions*, 5(2), 44–54. DOI: 10.1145/274430.274436. 25

Newman, D., Gall, N., and Lapkin, A. (2008). Gartner defines enterprise information architecture. Available at: https://online.ist.psu.edu/sites/ea/files/t5_gartner_defines_enterprise_i_154071.pdf. 3

Nielsen, J. (1993). Iterative user-interface design. *Computer*, 26(11), 32–41. DOI: 10.1109/2.241424. 37

Nielsen, J. (1995). 10 heuristics for user interface design. Retrieved December 24, 2016, from https://www.nngroup.com/articles/ten-usability-heuristics/.

Nielsen, J. (2006). F-shaped pattern for reading web content. Retrieved December 22, 2016, from https://www.nngroup.com/articles/f-shaped-pattern-reading-web-content/. 82

Nielsen, J. (2007). The myth of the genius designer. Retrieved December 21, 2016, from https://www.nngroup.com/articles/the-myth-of-the-genius-designer/. 122

Nielsen, J. (2012). How many test users in a usability study? Retrieved January 8, 2017, from https://www.nngroup.com/articles/how-many-test-users/. 55

Nielsen, J. and Mack, R. L. (1994). *Usability Inspection Methods*. Wiley and Sons:New York. DOI: 10.1145/259963.260531. 51

Nielsen, J. and Loranger, H. (2006). *Prioritizing Web Usability*. New Riders Press. 84

NISO. (2004). *Understanding Metadata*. Bethesda MD: NISO Press. Retrieved from http://www.niso.org/publications/press/UnderstandingMetadata.pdf. 60

Norman, D. (1998). *The Design of Everyday Things*. Basic Books. 90, 91

Norman, D. (2002). Beyond the computer industry. *Communications of the ACM*, 45(7), 120–. DOI: 10.1145/514236.514269. 26

Nylander, S., Lundquist, T., and Brännström, A. (2009). At home and with computer access: why and where people use cell phones to access the internet. In *Proceedings of the SIGCHI Conference on Human Factors in Computing Systems* (pp. 1639–1642). ACM. DOI: 10.1145/1518701.1518951. 108

Petty, R. E. and Cacioppo, J. T. (1986). The elaboration likelihood model of persuasion. *Advances in Experimental Social Psychology*, 19, 123–205. DOI: 10.1016/S0065-2601(08)60214-2. 78

Pew Research Center. (2014). *Three Technology Revolutions*. Pew Research Center. Retrieved from http://www.pewinternet.org/three-technology-revolutions/. 107

Pew Research Center. (2016). *Internet Users Predominate across Regions, Except in Africa*. Retrieved from http://www.pewglobal.org/2016/02/22/internet-access-growing-worldwide-but-remains-higher-in-advanced-economies/technology-report-02-07/. 130

Pirolli, P., and Card, S. (1999). Information foraging. *Psychological Review*, 106(4), 643. DOI: 10.1037/0033-295X.106.4.643. 77

Plattner, H., Meinel, C., and Leifer, L. (2016). *Design Thinking Research: Taking Breakthrough Innovation Home* (1st ed.). Springer Publishing Company, Incorporated. 26

Poushter, J. (2016). *Smartphone Ownership and Internet Usage Continues to Climb in Emerging Economies*. Retrieved from http://www.pewglobal.org/2016/02/22/smartphone-ownership-and-internet-usage-continues-to-climb-in-emerging-economies/. 18

Pruitt, J. and Grudin, J. (2003). Personas: practice and theory. In *Proceedings of the 2003 Conference on Designing for User Experiences* (pp. 1–15). ACM:New York. DOI: 10.1145/997078.997089. 26, 49

Reda, R. (2014). *Why UX Designers Need to Think like Architects*. Available at: https://uxmag.com/articles/why-ux-designers-need-to-think-like-architects. 5

Resmini, A. and Rosati, L. (2011). *Pervasive Information Architecture: Designing Cross-Channel User Experiences*. Elsevier. DOI: 10.1109/tpc.2011.2170911. 2, 10

Ries, E. (2011). *The Lean Startup: How Today's Entrepreneurs Use Continuous Innovation to Create Radically Successful Businesses*. Crown Books. 121

Rodriguez, A. (2008). *Restful Web Services: The Basics*. IBM developerWorks. 14

Rosch, E. H. (1973). Natural categories. *Cognitive Psychology*, 4(3), 328–350. DOI: 10.1016/0010-0285(73)90017-0. 80

Rosenfeld, L., Morville, P., and Arango, J. (2015). *Information Architecture* (4th ed.). O'Reilly Media. Retrieved from http://shop.oreilly.com/product/0636920034674.do. 2, 42

Ross, J. (2014). *The Business Value of User Experience. D3 Infragistics*. Retrieved from http://d3.infragistics.com/wp-content/uploads/2015/07/The_Business_Value_of_User_Experience1.pdf. 26

S.272 - High-Performance Computing Act of 1991. S.272 - High-Performance Computing Act of 1991 (1991). Retrieved from https://www.congress.gov/bill/102nd-congress/senate-bill/272. 12

Sauro, J. (2013). A brief history of usability: MeasuringU. Retrieved December 11, 2016, from http://www.measuringu.com/blog/usability-history.php. 25

Sauro, J. and Lewis, J. (2016). *Quantifying the User Experience* (2nd ed.). Cambridge, MA: Morgan Kaufmann. Retrieved from https://books.google.com/books/about/Quantifying_the_User_Experience.html?id=USPfCQAAQBAJ. 30, 47

Schwartz, B. (2004). *The Paradox of Choice*. Ecco:New York. 79

Simon, H. (1996). *The Sciences of the Artificial* (3rd ed.). MIT Press:Cambridge, MA. 78

Sinha, R. (2005). *A Cognitive Analysis of Tagging*. Retrieved December 17, 2016, from https://rashmisinha.com/2005/09/27/a-cognitive-analysis-of-tagging/. 66

Spink, A. and Cole, C. (2006). Human information behavior: Integrating diverse approaches and information use. *Journal of the American Society for Information Science and Technology*, 57(1), 25–35. DOI: 10.1002/asi.20249.

Spink, A. and Jansen, B. (2004). *Searching the Web: The Public and their Queries*. Springer. 84

Springer, M., Dulabahn, B., Michel, P., Natanson, B., Reser, D., Woodward, D., and Zinkham, H. (2008). *For the Common Good: The Library of Congress Flickr Pilot Project*. Library of Congress. Retrieved from http://www.loc.gov/rr/print/flickr_report_final.pdf. 66

Spohrer, J. (2016). T-shaped individuals: An imperative for industry. Presented at the UIDP. http://www.slideshare.net/spohrer/t-shaped-webinar-for-uidp-011915. 115

Spool, J. (2006). We are not alone, IA Summit '06 presentation. https://www.uie.com/brainsparks/2006/03/28/ia-summit-presentation-we-are-not-alone/. 114

Stanford University Institute of Design. (2016). *Use Our Methods*. Retrieved December 19, 2016, from http://dschool.stanford.edu/use-our-methods/. 121

Statsitica. (2016). *App Stores: Number of Apps in Leading App Stores 2016*. Retrieved December 10, 2016, from https://www.statista.com/statistics/276623/number-of-apps-available-in-leading-app-stores/. 110

Stokes, D. E. (1997). *Pasteur's Quadrant: Basic Science and Technological Innovation*. Brookings Institution Press. 140

Sun, H. (2001). Building a culturally-competent corporate website: an exploratory study of cultural markers in multilingual web design. In *Proceedings of the 19th Annual International Conference on Computer Documentation* (pp. 95–102). ACM. DOI: 10.1145/501516.501536. 133

The World Bank. (2015). Internet users (per 100 people) | Data. Retrieved December 18, 2016, from http://data.worldbank.org/indicator/IT.NET.USER.P2?end=2015&start=2015&view=map&year_high_desc=false. 129

Tognazzini, B. (2001). *Maximizing Human Performance*. Retrieved from http://www.asktog.com/basics/03Performance.html. 91, 92

Toub, S. (2000). *Evaluating Information Architecture: A Practical Guide to Assessing Website Organization*. Argus Center for Information Architecture. 51

Trant, J. (2009). Studying social tagging and folksonomy: A review and framework. *Journal of Digital Information*, 10(1). Retrieved from http://journals.tdl.org/jodi/article/view/269/278. 65

Tunkelang, D. (2009). Faceted search. *Synthesis Lectures on Information Concepts, Retrieval, and Services*, Morgan & Claypool Publishers, 1(1), 1–80. DOI: 10.2200/S00190ED1V01Y200904ICR005. 32, 64

United Nations General Assembly. (2012, June 29). Human Rights Council Twentieth Session - A/HRC/20/L.13. United Nations. Retrieved from https://documents-dds-ny.un.org/doc/UNDOC/LTD/G12/147/10/PDF/G1214710.pdf?OpenElement. 9

W3C. (2000). *A Little History of the World Wide Web*. Retrieved December 10, 2016, from https://www.w3.org/History.html. 10

Weiser, M. (1991). The computer for the 21st century. *Scientific American*, 265(3), 94–104. DOI: 10.1038/scientificamerican0991-94. 21

Whitten, J. L., Bentley, L. D., and Dittman, K. C. (2004). *Systems Analysis and Design Methods* (6th ed.). McGraw-Hill, Inc:New York. 26

Wilson, T. D. (2000). Human information behavior. *Informing Science*, 3(2), 49–56. 75

Wroblewski, L. (2012). *Mobile First*. A Book Apart. 107

Wurman, R. (1996). Information Architects, *Graphics Inc.* (October 1997). 1

Würtz, E. (2005). A cross-cultural analysis of websites from high-context cultures and low-context cultures. *Journal of Computer-Mediated Communication*, 11(1). 131

Yahoo! (n.d.). What's a Pattern - Design Pattern Library - YDN. Retrieved December 26, 2016, from https://developer.yahoo.com/ypatterns/everything.html. 102

Yu, J., Benatallah, B., Casati, F., and Daniel, F. (2008). Understanding mashup development. *IEEE Internet Computing*, 12(5), 44–52. DOI: 10.1109/MIC.2008.114. 13

Zarro, M. (2015). It's All Sales, Selling and Defending UX. Design presented at the PhillyCHI workshop series, Temple University. Retrieved from http://www.slideshare.net/mzarro/ux-and-ia-its-all-sales. 122

Zarro, M. and Carvin, M. (2011). User experience research: Is there an academic – practitioner divide? Internet presented at the *ACM SIGCHI Chapter* (PhillyCHI), Drexel University. Retrieved from http://www.slideshare.net/mzarro/user-experience-research-is-there-an-academic-practitioner-divide. 140

Zarro, M. and Hall, C. (2012). Exploring social curation. *D-Lib Magazine*, 18(11/12). DOI: 10.1045/november2012-zarro. 65

Zipf, G. K. (1949). *Human Behavior and the Principle of Least Effort: An Introduction to Human Ecology*. Addison-Wesley. 77

Author Biographies

Dr. Wei Ding is a digital product strategist and program manager with more than 20 years of experience in user experience design, marketing, and consumer behavior. She is currently leading the digital product team at the U.S. Consumer Financial Protection Bureau (CFPB), overseeing the ideation, design, and development of all consumer-facing digital products. Previously she held various design leadership positions at other federal government agencies and private sectors, including the Federal Aviation Administration, U.S. Patent and Trademark Office, Marriott International, and Vanguard. She helped institutions establish user experience design disciplines, and led the successful design/redesign of large-scaled ecommerce or government websites, such as uspto.gov, Marriott.com, and vanguard.com.

Dr. Ding has been an adjunct professor at Drexel University teaching Information Architecture and other graduate level courses since 2006. She has a Ph.D. degree in Information Science from the University of Maryland, and a B.S. and M.S. from Peking (Beijing) University. She has published a number of research papers and articles and is a frequent speaker at professional conferences and industry forums.

Dr. Xia Lin is a Professor in the College of Computing and Informatics at Drexel University. His major research areas include digital libraries, information visualization, information retrieval, and knowledge organization. He initiated the Information Architecture course at Drexel in 2003 and has taught the course for many years.

Dr. Lin has published more than 100 research papers and received significant research grants from federal agencies and industries. His visualization prototypes have been presented and demonstrated in many national and international conferences. Dr. Lin has a Ph.D. in Information Science from the University of Maryland at College Park and a Master of Librarianship from Emory University at Atlanta, Georgia. Prior to join Drexel, Dr. Lin was an assistant professor at the University of Kentucky.

Dr. Michael Zarro is a User Experience consultant with over 15 years experience leading UX projects for some of the largest technology companies in the world. Currently he manages an international customer research practice for the Project Management Institute. Previously, he taught graduate-level Information Architecture courses at Drexel University, supervised a Master's Thesis at the University of the Arts in Philadelphia, and taught in a technology learning program at Bryn Mawr College.

Dr. Zarro has a Ph.D. in information science from Drexel University, and an MSLIS also from Drexel. He has managed UX research projects around the globe, from the wilds of Alaska to a banking center of Germany. Dr. Zarro designed one of the first product subscription services in eCommerce, and conducted some of the earliest research on social curation. He has published over a dozen research papers and articles, and presented his work at leading international conferences.